To
Jamila,

It's been a heck of a
ride! Want to share
it with you.
Thank you in advance!

RAISING THE STEAKS

MY JOURNEY TO CREATING THE BEST STEAKHOUSE IN THE WORLD: NICK & SAM'S

RAISING THE STEAKS

MY JOURNEY TO CREATING THE BEST
STEAKHOUSE IN THE WORLD: NICK & SAM'S

SAMIR DHURANDHAR
with Steve McLinden

Favorite Recipes® Press

Raising the Steaks was edited, designed, and manufactured by Favorite Recipes Press in collaboration with Samir Dhurandhar. Favorite Recipes Press works with top chefs, food and appliance manufacturers, restaurants and resorts, health organizations, Junior Leagues, and nonprofit organizations to create award-winning cookbooks and other food-related products. Favorite Recipes Press is an imprint of Southwestern Publishing House, Inc., 2451 Atrium Way, Nashville, Tennessee, 37214. Southwestern Publishing House is a wholly owned subsidary of Southwestern/Great American, Inc., Nashville, Tennessee.

Christopher G. Capen, President, Southwestern Publishing House
Sheila Smith, Publisher, Favorite Recipes Press
Vicky Shea, Senior Art Director
Kristin Connelly, Managing Editor
Linda Brock, Proofreader
swpublishinghouse.com | 800-358-0560

Photo Credits (left to right, top to bottom):
Images from the personal collection of Samir Dhurandhar: pp. 14, 22, 29, 38, 41, 42, 44, 47, 49a, 49b, 51, 53, 54, 56, 64, 66, 68a, 68b, 69, 73, 82, 84, 87, 92, 99, 105, 111, 112, 116, 119

© Lara Bierner: Cover, back flap, p. 156; © Brandon Colston Photography: pp. 48, 91, 100; © Lee Lockwood/Getty Images: p. 34; © Rina Oh/James Beard House: p. 58; Courtesy of the Mavs: p. 46; © Monika Normand/The Nix Company: pp. 2-3, 4, 6-7, 10, 11-12, 17, 18, 20, 23, 24, 25, 26, 27, 32, 52, 59, 71, 78, 79, 80, 83, 86, 96, 114, 121, 122, 155; © Sam Hazen: p. 109; © White Unicorn Agency: p. 16a, 16b; Grilling Utensils Icon © bubaone/istock

ISBN: 978-0-87197-613-0

Library of Congress Control Number: 2023902045

Printed in China
10 9 8 7 6 5 4 3 2 1

Dedication

I dedicate this book to the chef in India who once told me: "Young man, you will never make it in this business." Thank you for the inspiration and the drive that got me to where I am today.

Special gratitude goes to my children, Mia and Cole, who have been constant sources of encouragement and support during the writing of this book and in everyday life.

To my wife, Lori: Thank you for accepting me as me, for supporting my ambition, my dreams, and my hustle. You will always be my perfect wife and the perfect mother to our children.

Thank you to my parents, Taru and Kanu, and my siblings, Kavita and Prasanna. Your good examples have taught me to achieve more than I could have ever imagined.

And a special thank you to Philip Romano, who helped mold me as a person and gave me the freedom to create. Thanks for your wisdom, inspiration, guidance, knowledge, and understanding.

Finally, I dedicate this book to everyone who wonders if I am writing about them . . . I am!

Contents

FOREWORD BY DIRK NOWITZKI 15

ACKNOWLEDGMENT 19

CHAPTER 1   A Night at Nick & Sam's 21

CHAPTER 2   "Samir, This Is Julia Child" 33

CHAPTER 3   Celebs, Super Fans, Superb Wine 43

CHAPTER 4   Honor of a Lifetime: Cooking at the
James Beard House 57

CHAPTER 5   Strange Tales from the Kitchen 73

CHAPTER 6   Dishing with Samir 81

CHAPTER 7   The Founder's Tale (and other takes) 101

CHAPTER 8   A Toast to My Two Families 115

RECIPES BY SAMIR 123

ABOUT THE AUTHOR 157

INDEX 159

Foreword

I first met my friend Samir Dhurandhar during the Dallas Mavericks' 2000 season. It was only my second year in Dallas and the NBA, and I was still learning about my new home. I love good food, and I am always looking for great places to eat. That's how I found Samir.

We clicked instantly. Both new to the USA at the time, we each came to town at a young age with big dreams—me from Germany and Samir from India—each determined to work hard and succeed.

As our journeys progressed over the years, we became great friends. We celebrated our successes and shared our disappointments. What I learned from Samir was his natural ability to make people feel good about themselves—from his coworkers to his guests. I admired his work ethic and boundless energy.

Immediately, I recognized we were living similar team experiences. Samir's restaurant, Nick & Sam's, has a great team. Success comes from putting leaders and talent in the right place at the right time. And Samir is that leader who instills preparation and a winning mindset in every team member. He demands communication and togetherness but always encourages individual creativity as well.

Samir is not just an executive chef. He does it all—owner, GM, chef, server, and marketing and PR manager all rolled into one. He's always looking for ways to innovate and to help his players up their game and max out their talents. His strong leadership guarantees an amazing and memorable experience every time a customer walks through the door.

Dirk Nowitzki and Samir

Samir never rests; his impact goes far beyond his restaurants. The man has been loyal and so generous to me and the Dirk Nowitzki Foundation. From catered luncheons to food donations to cooking demos, he's all in. He and I worked together to organize a Mother's Day food drive during the COVID-19 crisis. We helped feed over 2,000 people thanks to Samir.

I leave you with one final Samir story. In November of 2017, Samir and my wife secretly planned a "surprise" party in my honor. I arrived to find my team-mates, friends, and Samir, who took the occasion to announce he was adding a new item to the menu—"The Dirk," a 41-ounce tenderloin aged for 41 days—in honor of my Mavericks number, 41. The room erupted in applause as everyone was served "The Dirk." It was truly a night I will never forget.

But that's Samir for you.

For me and for all who know him, Samir is a superstar. And he's a true MVP in business and in his personal life. I'm honored to call him my friend.

Samir, I'm giving you 5 Stars.

-41-

Acknowledgment

I'd like to thank my cowriter, Steve McLinden, for his patience, organization, ideas, and research in helping me bring these recollections to life and for aiding me in pulling together and formatting some of my favorite recipes and kitchen tips.

McLinden is a Peoria, IL–based writer, who coauthored two books for restaurateur Phil Romano: *Food for Thought: How the Creator of Fuddruckers, Romano's Macaroni Grill, and eatZi's Built a $10 Billion Empire One Concept at a Time* and *The Mad Entrepreneur: Making a Difference in the World, in Business and in Life.* He also cowrote *Summerall: On and Off the Air* with sportscasting great Pat Summerall and *Diversity: Leaders Not Labels—A New Plan for the 21st Century* with educator Stedman Graham.

McLinden is a contributing editor of ICSC's *Commerce+Communities Today.*

CHAPTER 1

A Night at Nick & Sam's

It's Saturday night, and it's insanely busy at the hottest—and coolest— steakhouse in Dallas: Nick & Sam's. Celebratory shouts and laughs ring out through our dining room over the clatter of plates, silverware, happy talk, and live piano music.

I love to pause just past the kitchen exit to our dining room to drink in the rich atmosphere of this magical place, where I've spent the last twenty-four years of my life. After all that time, it's still an absolute joy to watch our guests get pampered.

By way of introduction, I am Samir Dhurandhar (dhu-rand-har), a native of India and Nick & Sam's executive chef and partner. I have managed the kitchen at this iconic place since it opened in 1999 and became a co-owner a few years later. Of the staff who started with me, two-thirds are still here. Like our guests, our people find it hard to leave this place.

For me, it's been a dream come true and an American success story for a kid who struggled mightily through school on the other side of the world. Most folks here just call me "boss," but my partners and a few others call me "C.C." (celebrity chef). I don't see myself as a celebrity; our guests are the real celebrities!

While we attract a diversified and multigenerational crowd, we are never wanting for beautiful people. The hundreds of television and movie stars, pro athletes, broadcasters, and the like who have passed through our doors arrive at our hotspot by word-of-mouth—literally. George Clooney dines here when in town. So does Shaq O'Neill, Diddy, Bono, Jimmy Kimmel, Jaime Foxx, Emma Watson, and Derek Jeter to name just a very few. We can't forget all of the former Dallas Cowboys we see regularly, including all-time greats Roger Staubach, Troy Aikman, Emmitt Smith, Michael Irvin, and Tony Romo. (Tony raved about a specialty cake I made him.)

We've also served The Black-Eyed Peas—the band not the food. It would take chapters to mention all the "who's who." But we'll get back to those other A-listers later.

While patrons come here to enjoy what one reviewer describes as our "upscale but not uptight" atmosphere, our food is the main attraction and the true star of the show. This is the kind of place where Frank Sinatra and the Rat Pack would have hung out back in the day.

David Holben, Roger Staubach, Samir, and team

Like players in a Broadway production, our staff's movements are perfectly practiced and choreographed, their dialogue flows smoothly, and their entrances and exits are perfectly timed. It's obvious from the purpose in their steps and their eagerness to please that our supporting cast has wholly bought into Nick & Sam's founding vision: Take care of the customer.

The element of surprise also sets us apart. Some surprises unfold right in front of my eyes as I pause to observe. One of our guests is having a birthday just a few tables away. In fact, we've become *the* birthday-dinner destination in Dallas for those seeking an unforgettable night out. And there are a bunch of parties tonight. Confetti flies, champagne flows, and our "rising-smoke" effect, which we get from pouring hot water over dry ice, wows the table.

The huge, puffy cloud of cotton candy that we serve for birthdays, which arrived at the table just after dinner, has already been picked clean. But here comes the crowning touch: the tallest five-layer, five-flavor cake you'll ever find. It was baked fresh, layer by painstaking layer, in our kitchen this morning and is served topped with lit sparklers instead of candles! It's a showstopper. Nick & Sam's is both the steak *and* the sizzle.

At another table, our legendary sides are starting to emerge: Lobster Deviled Eggs, Oysters Rockefeller, and Hokkaido Scallops, as is our savory treatment of Foie Gras, accompanied by roasted peaches and brown butter crumble. Several have opted for the beautifully simple "Damn" Good Fries. Yes, they are as good as advertised!

I see that a group across from the birthday table is now onto their main courses. There's our Dry Aged "Long Bone" Cowboy Steak served in black truffle butter, our Butter Poached Halibut, our Mangalitsa Pork Chop, and our great Kobe Ribeye. The table is splitting an order of Kung Pao Lobster, one of my favorites. Often overheard after a plate of Nick & Sam's food arrives: "This shit is going to be delicious."

In a booth against the wall, at least one guest I see is dining like a Japanese emperor tonight, knifing into our succulent Ohmi Beef Tenderloin. Ohmi sits at the very top of Japan's strict beef-marbling scale with an "A-5" ranking. It comes from a line of the "black cattle" raised for centuries in Japan's Shiga Prefecture along Lake Biwa. To the shogun, this beef is said to be like a treasured gift. Ohmi, oh my!

The satisfied smile on this emperor-for-a-night's face reflects the steak's melt-in-your-mouth tenderness and its smooth, almost sweet flavor, which can't be found anywhere else in this seven-million-plus population region other than at

Nick & Sam's. Just a handful of restaurants in the USA serve it. Of course, it is a delicacy and a rare one at that. This probably goes without saying, but at around $70 an ounce, Ohmi is just one of eight different cuts of "Wagyu" Japanese steak we're known for. (Let's get this out of the way now: This Indian native IS an avid meat eater. Thank you.)

Near where I now stand, there's a classic grand piano in play, but no, it's not in our private dining hall. Of all places, it sits on the dining-room side of the open kitchen for all to enjoy. Tickle those ivories. Unconventional? Of course!

Over the years, I've seen a few newbie servers who are already struggling to balance trays of food get thrown off by that piano jutting out into what would ordinarily be the natural pathway to our dining room, which creates the kind of end clatter that always draws sarcastic applause in a restaurant. But the mostly veteran staff jukes around it with practiced ease.

My good friend, the now-retired Dallas Maverick star Dirk Nowitzki, is at his favorite private table tonight, trying to keep a low profile, as if a seven-foot-tall surefire NBA Hall of Famer can actually do that. Most Dallas-area pro athletes past and present come here packing mammoth appetites, and our huge servings don't disappoint. We routinely serve the athletes even after our regular quitting time if they'll let us know they're on the way.

A new Mavs mega-superstar, Luka Dončić, even gave us an *in-game shout-out* in a sideline interview during the Rising Stars game at the 2020 NBA All-Star weekend in Chicago. TNT announcer Myles Turner asked Luka what he did with his free time in Dallas, and Luka quickly replied, "I go to Nick & Sam's." The announcer chuckled and responded, "Ah, that's a good spot." Luka was even thinking of us during a pro basketball game more than 1,000 miles away! He was an All-Star again in 2021, 2022, and 2023.

This restaurant's founder, Phil Romano, is here tonight with his grown son, Sam, a Syracuse grad and the same "Sam" who inspired the latter half of Nick & Sam's name. He took over as our majority owner and general partner in early 2022. Phil, the restaurant industry's most prolific creator of national concepts, such as Romano's Macaroni Grill, Fuddruckers, Rudy's Country Store and Bar-B-Q, eatZi's, and more than a couple dozen others, is our resident celebrity.

Phil rescued this piece of real estate at 3008 Maple Avenue in Uptown Dallas back in 1998 and recast it into one of the prime steakhouses in the Southwest less than a year later. For a quarter century, the building housed the reliable but somber Lawry's The Prime Rib. Before that, it was a morgue. The place needed some reanimation, and it got that in abundance.

The walls are decked with energetic, larger-than-life paintings, many crafted by artist Phil, who late in life indulged another of his natural talents to open one of the premiere art galleries in the region, Samuel Lynne Galleries. One of Phil's paintings, the vivid, wall-length *Integration*, is on permanent display on the University of

Nevada Las Vegas campus. Also, lively art deco–style murals from different artists adorn the restaurant.

The posh bar along the north wall behind me is full of young dressed-to-impress patrons, mixing with our regulars and newer guests—some nibbling on the free caviar we serve from our caviar trolley and some sipping on a concoction such as a Cabana, with rum, pineapple, and house-made coconut syrup or the potent Oaxaca, with Añejo Tequila and mezcal. There are sexy, striking photos from noted photographers on the wall.

As I look out over this great dining hall, I realize I've never felt so right being anywhere else. It was as if I was born to do exactly what I do and where I do it. Most executive chefs typically come in late afternoon, tend to administrative chores and maybe a little prep work, and then head home to cool their heels. Not me. I love to be here—I *should* be here—to take care of business and make sure we cater to our guests' every whim.

If one of our esteemed customers happens to want something that we don't offer on the menu, I may just dash out to my car and speed to the store to get the ingredients and then cook it myself, as I've done on countless occasions. Even at this stage of my career, I continue to learn something new every day. If I'm not here, what would I miss?

It's now getting on 9 p.m. Lori, my wife, will be expecting me. She keeps asking, "Isn't this supposed to get easier for you, Samir?" But she knows I am heavily invested in this grand place in every sense of the word and am a doer, so I don't do "easy." She loves coming here, too.

I have the luxury of basking in the sights and sounds and smells of our iconic dining hall as I stand here for these few minutes because I know my amazing sous chefs, cooks, and other staff have my back. Now, it's time to get back to what I do best.

But how did I get to this festive eating place deep in the heart of Texas steak country, some 8,700 miles from my Indian birthplace? It's a journey worth retracing.

I was born in New Delhi on July 22, 1968, but actually grew up in another Indian megalopolis, Bombay, now known as Mumbai, where my family moved when I was little. It was my lovely mother, Taru, whose exquisite culinary gifts grew to become legendary in our part of town, who really opened my eyes to the fine art of cooking. A master chef herself, she piqued my interest in this art form when I was at a tender age.

Thoughts of her transport me to the dinner table of my youth, with all the diverse and colorful dishes of my homeland. I can almost see and taste her cooking now: those generous spreads of four delicious proteins and four vegetables that she lovingly prepared nightly for our family of five. What a sensory delight!

Ah, I can just imagine them now. There are her famous potato-crusted lamb chops braised in vinegar, roasted goat, and sumptuous Bombay-style fried shrimp, which I always made disappear like magic. And there's her exquisite sambar, a finely finessed Indian vegetable and lentil stew, plus her spinach-braised

Samir and Lori with Samir's parents, Taru and Kanu Dhurandhar, and Shauna, Kavita, and Rehan Gonsalves

mutton and the regional, curiously named crumbly delicacy called "Bombay duck," which isn't duck at all. It's really a small lizardfish found only in the briny waters around Mumbai.

On other days, we devoured chicken with sweet peas and caramel, crepe shrimp with heaping serving plates of fresh okra, corn, and peas, and sometimes something exotic like fried brains. Confession: The fried brains she cooked were probably the best thing I ever ate.

All of these uncommonly delicious dishes still beckon me so many years later. I will share some of mom's creative recipes with you on these pages. (Okay, maybe not the fried brains.)

As word of her kitchen skills spread around our neighborhood, mom began hosting more and more cooking classes at our home. And I always volunteered to help. She'd rub my head and call me her "little sous chef." As a kid, I ate that up almost as much as I did her cooking, which was more than compensation for my efforts. If not a cooking class, there was always some sort of celebration going on at our home, and the constant exotic aromas tantalized me. As any conscientious sous chef—and good son—would do, I took it upon myself to sample her work throughout the day as I learned her recipe secrets.

It was our good fortune to live in a fashionable area of town called Juhu, which had become a Mumbai destination of sorts, with its beachfront properties. I understand parts of it are now home to Bollywood stars. As I grew, I would venture out with my buddies into our vast and colorful city to enjoy its sights, tastes, and sports fields. There were about eighteen of us in my core group of friends from the two twelve-story apartment buildings that comprised our complex, enough to field full soccer and cricket teams for tournaments and leagues, which we did frequently, both on our fields and around town.

I guess that's one reason why I wasn't a very good student. With my penchant for sports, my frequent beach going, and general daydreaming, school was almost an afterthought; it was always a big struggle for me.

It got so bad that I had to forge my parents' signatures on my report cards. I even failed ninth grade for lack of serious study, then concealed that, and lied to my parents about other things in my youth. Every time I was caught in a fib, my mother would put hot green chili peppers in my mouth as punishment. I didn't dare tell her that I was starting to enjoy them. Today, I still eat hot peppers raw! I did represent my school well in one thing: ping-pong competition. To this day, I am sort of a ping-pong—and peppers—wiz.

But wherever I was and wherever my two older sisters were, my dear father, Kanu, insisted that we all gather together for dinner each night. "I don't care what you're doing, but at 8 o'clock in the evening, we will meet at this dining table and have dinner together, whether we speak a word or not to one another," he'd say with authority. So, no matter what occupied us, we dropped what we were doing and made our way home to dine at the best supper table in Mumbai. And sure enough, minutes after we dug into our feast, the lively chatter began.

One night, the happy talk turned to gloom when my father asked me how tenth grade was treating me. I almost choked on a mouthful of food. I looked at him with puppy eyes and said, "I wouldn't know, dad, because I am still in the ninth." He turned as red as tandoori chicken. Gulp!

Though this turn of events surely didn't boost his confidence in me, my father was always a reasonable man, and he eventually forgave me. He had a lot on his mind as a higher-up with the Esso company, which was then India's Exxon oil brand.

Dad studied business management at UCLA, and he and mom taught us English as a first language, though we also learned Hindi and Marathi. The latter was my state tongue and just two of India's more than 700 distinct languages.

Ironically, dad was later recruited to the food business by conglomerate Parle Products, where he eventually became CEO. Under his direction, Parle launched the Thums Up cola soft drink, which basically became the Coca-Cola of India, since Coke had temporarily pulled out of the country due to foreign-investment restrictions. I guess you could say my dad was a pretty enterprising fellow.

But he made it home for dinner every night, no matter how busy he was. Over the years, he helped us remain a very close-knit family, which is one of the main cultural differences in my upbringing compared to the West, where families tend to be splintered in so many different directions.

As I look back, our family dinners weren't just festive gatherings; they were rituals of nourishment and togetherness in both physical and spiritual realms, lovingly prepared offerings of savory tastes that would bring us great memories not just sustenance. That ethic lives on in me as I prepare food for my own family and for my restaurant guests at Nick & Sam's. They're always "home for dinner" in my eyes.

But how did a poorly educated Indian man end up as the executive chef at one of the most prominent steakhouses in the world?

CHAPTER 2

"Samir, This Is Julia Child"

After years of hearing his enthusiastic tales about the wonders of the USA, my father finally brought our entire family over to the states for a coast-to-coast trip. We traveled first to Disney World in Orlando and finished in Santa Barbara, California, not far from his old UCLA stomping grounds. While in Santa Barbara, we stayed with one of dad's dearest and longest-term friends, Robert Huttenback, or "Uncle Bob" as we called him in the endearing Indian tradition of addressing elder family friends as "uncle" and "aunty."

Uncle Bob had a lovely backyard swimming pool, which I was floating in one morning, daydreaming deeply, of course, when Bob suddenly appeared poolside. "Can you come to the kitchen real quick, Samir?" he asked. "I want you to meet someone."

I dried off hastily and headed inside. "What is this?" I wondered. As I walked in the kitchen, I sensed a commanding presence. There, standing next to Uncle Bob was a distinguished-looking middle-aged woman. Smartly dressed and statuesque, she had to have stood more than six feet tall. "Samir, do you know who this is?" Bob asked. With curious eyes, I stared up at the woman, but I just couldn't place her. I sheepishly responded, "I apologize, I don't." Bob said, "Samir, this is

Julia Child." As in *the* Julia Child, the famous chef, cooking educator, television personality, and author of the world-renowned cooking bible *Mastering the Art of French Cooking*, among other magnificent cooking books. Of course, I didn't realize any of this at the time. I was simply told that she lived in nearby Pasadena, was a friend of Uncle Bob's family, and was very influential, but that's it.

Julia and I sat and talked for the longest time. That "real quick" meeting that Uncle Bob had summoned me for had turned into an hour-and-a-half heart-to-heart talk. We discussed family and life in general in addition to cooking, of course. Julia was very easy to speak with and came off as unpretentious, smart,

James Beard and Julia Child

and perceptive. I found out later that she'd been a top-secret researcher in World War II for America's Office of Strategic Services. Wow!

I don't recall many specifics of our conversation, but I remember her asking me to share my passion for food with her. And that I did, in my own awkward way. I remember feeling a little embarrassed about the mumbo-jumbo that I was spouting. I was a twenty-one-year-old "kid" who was still a little wet behind the ears, doubly so after my interrupted dip in the pool.

But Julia gracefully indulged my youthful spirit. Although I had prepared meals for my family as a kid and worked for a while as a junior sous chef at the Sheraton Hotel in Mumbai, I had very little professional experience. But as we spoke, I think Julia recognized that my passion for cooking was not only genuine, but also it ran deep, especially as I recollected my mother's guiding influence and inherited passion for distinctive foods. I'm sure she saw my face light up as we discussed the art and craft of preparing creative and nutritious meals.

As I reflect, it was a seminal moment in my life. After that, everything started coming together. The one big thing holding me back in my formative schooling had been my lack of direction. But here I was, starting to see a much clearer purpose for my life—happily one that dovetailed with my passion for cooking.

Julia told me, "Samir, if you are interested in this as a career, you should go to the Culinary Institute of America." She seemed sure I would get in, so I followed her advice. On my return to Mumbai, my desire to be a great chef had not faded in the least; it was hitting a fever pitch. The thought of doing something that I love as a vocation really elevated my spirit. So, I applied to the Culinary Institute of Hyde Park, New York, USA, with the blessing of both of my parents and was soon delighted to learn that I had gained acceptance for the very next school year, starting in fall 1990.

As I've said, it never fully hit me when I met her what a big deal Julia Child was to the culinary world—that is, until I got to the Culinary Institute of America (we called it the CIA), the first school to formally teach the culinary arts in the states. Julia was like a rock star there, idolized by its staff, students, and graduates. What's more, our paths were destined to cross again.

Culinary school was challenging at first to say the least. The biggest obstacle facing me was adaptation. So many people tend to resist adapting when they find themselves in a foreign country or a place outside their comfort zone. But I was determined to learn the culture, the food, the night spots, the slang, and the finer points of American food preparation.

I was twenty-two years old when I first walked through the institute's doors and met my roommate, a naive sixteen-year-old American kid. As I entered our dorm room, the look on his face seemed to shout, "Oh, my God, I have to spend two semesters with *this* guy?!"

He saw me as a curiosity, with my dark skin, exotic accent, and "foreign" features and dress, so he started peppering me with questions, starting with where I was from. When I replied that I was from India, he responded, "Where's that?"

Where's that? Ha! Oh, boy, am I going to take this kid for a ride, I thought. I just might have to mess with him a little. So, as we spoke, I convinced him with a straight and solemn face that my father was the "king" of the western region of India and that I was a "prince." So thrilled to be the roommate of royalty, he told practically everyone in school my story. Soon, people in the hallways were bowing to me, and I must admit that I took my sweet time setting them straight. It's not often that you get to be a prince!

I was soon brought down to earth, humbled by my early class work, particularly in those first few weeks. I was especially challenged by what you could call "American food culture shock." I had spent virtually my entire life in India with minimal exposure to Western-style cooking and foodstuffs. And in just my third class, Purchasing and Receiving, instructors discovered my weakness. They had spread out a substantial variety of meats and vegetables and cooking ingredients on a big table and asked students to identify and list them. The problem was that I had never seen half of these things!

I couldn't identify the poblano pepper, for example, because I had grown up eating only green chilies such as the Kashmiri and Guntur varieties—sometimes for punishment! What's more, I had never seen red peppers, fennel, radicchio, rosemary, red cabbage, romaine, or iceberg lettuce, as well as an assortment of other items such as sushi. Needless to say, my food identity list was sparse, and I fared poorly in that early class, coming away with a "D" paper.

When I got my grade, a student sitting next to me leaned over, saw my paper, and immediately started laughing out loud. At the Culinary Institute, I was learning to rein in my youthful temper, but damn, that guy really pissed me off. But instead of lashing out or getting discouraged, I used the incident to motivate me. It was just the added impetus I needed to press harder and rein in those shortfalls to accelerate my learning curve. I vowed to stay in touch with this arrogant young man to compare how he progressed in his career and I in mine. I won't identify the student who made fun of me, but let's just say that my career path over the years has compared quite favorably to his.

I spent far more time learning these foods than anyone else in school. I would feel awkward going out with friends to places like a sushi bar, where I was clueless how to order. Through all of this, I had to take a step back and remind myself to adapt.

At this point, my eyes were wide open, and I gradually felt more at ease. Three months into the semester, the esteemed Julia Child, who had inspired my culinary-school adventure, entered the picture again. She was visiting with instructors on campus and was signing her many books for students. She drew quite a crowd.

By this time, I was beginning to grasp what a huge influence Julia had been on not only me but also the cooking world everywhere. Her career and creative influence had served to bring the great chefs of the world into the limelight at a time when we were largely considered back-room laborers. To this day, we can't thank Julia enough.

When I got to the front of the line and placed my book in front of her to sign, Julia glanced up from the table, smiled, and said, "Samir, how wonderful to see you!" The fact that she remembered me and our meeting in Uncle Bob's kitchen simply blew me away. More motivation!

By this time, that sense of higher purpose that had been germinating in me was really starting to bloom. I was slowly overcoming my cultural and professional barriers, mostly with hard work, careful observation, and yes, extra studying. The word "study" had evolved from a bad word in my vocabulary to an essential one.

Samir with his father, Kanu Dhurandhar, at the Culinary Institute of America

My work at the four public restaurants that the Culinary Institute operated to enable students to gain real-world experience was well regarded. Swelling with pride and determination, I was all set to graduate from this esteemed culinary school in 1993. Watch out world!

But reality struck again. There was one barrier yet to be overcome, and it was a huge one. To remain in America, I needed a job—and a green card.

The end of my culinary schooling was nearing, and I had my fingers crossed. The institute sponsored many career fairs to help place its students, and I was front and center at them. But I was a little different than the others: an Indian chef cooking American cuisine and meat. Who would take a chance on me?

But it was from that fair that kind fate arose. It was at one of the last fairs of the semester that I first met a rising talent, Richard Pietromonico, then corporate chef for Sfuzzi's in New York City. We hit it off instantly. Richard seemed to recognize my creative passion for cooking and appreciated the obstacles I had to overcome and the fact that I was well-grounded in my life goals and perspective. Plus, as it turned out, Richard had emerged from the same culinary institute some seven years earlier!

Soon after, Richard called with the fantastic news that he was willing to take a chance on me, and he made me an offer to work alongside him as a chef in Manhattan at the exciting US chain Sfuzzi's, which was fast gaining fame for its savory Italian food, big crowds, and strategic locations. Not only would I get my American work papers, but I'd also be launching my career in the Big Apple at the chain's flagship restaurant, situated directly across from the heavily trafficked Lincoln Center.

Richard even hinted that I'd have some creative latitude to conceive dishes of my own. That sort of thing was my dream! Armed with my degree, I took my knives, newfound skills, and youthful enthusiasm to New York to work under Richard.

Like me, Richard's affection for unique food started at a young age. As a kid, he would scoop up soft-shell crabs along Staten Island's docks and harvest fruits and veggies from his dad's unique and diverse backyard garden. He would then experiment on food combinations of his own.

In the absurdly busy Sfuzzi's kitchen, Richard turned out to be a thoughtful and patient mentor. He shrugged off my mistakes because he knew I would learn from them, and he took the time to show me the correct way in every respect to do everything in the kitchen. And most importantly, he showed me how to take care of the guests. Too many chefs seem to grow to have quiet contempt for the people they serve. Not Richard. Not me.

At this point, Sfuzzi's had grown into a corporate conglomerate, and there wasn't much room on the menu for individual inspiration. But Richard was true to his word about giving me creative latitude. To the chagrin of the other Sfuzzi's chefs, he let me modify the menu with my own creative flair. In fact, I've learned that I was the first Sfuzzi's chef in the entire coast-to-coast chain to individually create a menu.

That, too, was a learning experience. The larger lesson was that chefs can't simply cook what they want to cook. Just because a chef likes a dish doesn't mean guests will like it. And I made the mistake of putting a few things on the menu that they didn't want to eat. Some guests vowed they wouldn't come back because we did away with their favorites. Lesson learned.

In my mind, I had failed because I had made guests unhappy. And that's when I really learned to step back and determine what our customers—not me or other chefs—really wanted. In this world of constantly evolving competition, we need to take the time to listen to our guests. A lot of chefs with big egos never learn that.

Failure is never pleasant, but it was just the humbling that I needed to grow and thrive in this business. So, we tweaked the menu again, leaving on some of my better-selling additions, and we stayed extremely busy and remained the number-one Sfuzzi's in the chain—that is, until the Las Vegas location opened.

Samir, Chef Gerard Thompson, and Joe T. Garcia, three Texas culinary legends

Incidentally, it was at the New York Sfuzzi's that I met former Nick & Sam's partner Joe Palladino, who was hired away by Sfuzzi's founder, Patrick Columbo, to help him open a fine-dining steak destination that Patrick was creating in Dallas, along with the world's top restaurant creator, Phil Romano. I didn't know Phil then, but I had worked with Patrick for years and had kept up with him after he went out on his own post-Sfuzzi's.

At about that same time, Patrick called *me* to offer me the chef post at his grand new restaurant. Richard and I had both moved on from Sfuzzi's by then, and I was helping him run his John Harvard's Brew House restaurant in Long Island and Heartland Brewery on Broadway.

I had worked in New York for nine years, and it's no secret that it's an incredibly pricey place, even if you're gainfully employed. My bank account was thin, and I was ready for a new challenge. So, I thought, why not? After all, you never know what's going to pan out. Plus, I realized that Dallas was a less expensive (and warmer) place to live.

My instincts were telling me that this was the right move. So, I crammed my sparse belongings into my rickety green Honda Civic and, with only $60 in my account, drove more than 1,500 miles to the gateway of the sunny Southwest to make my fortune in steak country. It was the best drive I ever made.

CHAPTER 3

Celebs, Super Fans, Superb Wine

Matthew McConaughey, Derek Jeter, Don Henley, and Justin Bieber. They've joined the likes of the aforementioned Bono and George Clooney, among countless other notables, to break bread with us, sometimes slipping in the back door to avoid the fuss that follows them. Some of their visits were compelling or downright amusing—even poignant. Their tales will follow.

But first, let me clear the air. There was a point during Nick & Sam's first decade of operation when we questioned whether our high profilers would even have their favorite Dallas dining hub to kick around in for future shining, dining, and wining.

You see, while Nick & Sam's opened to exceptional crowds in 1999 and enjoyed other strong surges in our early years, business became spotty a few years later. While it's not uncommon for even the best of one-off concepts to lose a little luster after grandiose debuts, especially in sprawling areas such as DFW, which is dominated by restaurant chains and their heavy advertising budgets, it was nevertheless troubling.

Sure, we had our reliable cast of regulars, but new business was tailing off. Then came 2008–2009 and the dreaded Great Recession. By 2010, our weekdays were skewing soft, and we were posting only average weekly sales. This sort of trend is always a matter of grave concern to anybody who's been in the biz awhile, and that goes for my partners and yours truly. At the time, our brain trust had a combined ninety years of experience in the restaurant industry (Phil has been at it since 1965!), and we all knew the restaurant gods could be cruel to even the best concepts.

We added menu items, organized some events, and launched publicity campaigns, and these goosed things a bit. But sporadic vacant tables persisted even in the face of grand reviews. Was the Nick & Sam's party winding down?

Then came Super Bowl XLV.

Emmitt Smith, Troy Aikman, Samir, and Michael Irvin

In 2011, the brand-new Dallas Cowboys stadium had lured the big game to neighboring Arlington for the first Sunday in February, and we naturally expected at least a little sales bump. If history served as a guide, there would be a substantial number of movers and shakers, high-profile current and former athletes, and otherwise beautiful people flocking to town early to populate the hot spots. Plus, the matchup between the storied Green Bay Packers and Pittsburgh Steelers franchises was a huge draw in itself.

Then, just as these super consumers were arriving by the jet load, the normally mild North Texas weather turned hostile. We got hit by an unusually bad ice storm early that week. A couple inches of the stuff was solidified even more by two subfreezing days and then topped off by about a half foot of snow mixed with sleet. What a mess!

Suddenly, the landscape looked more like Green Bay than Dallas. The slick and poorly plowed roads dampened fan access to pre-Super Bowl events. Many fans didn't venture too far from their hotels, but they still had to eat.

And eat they did—with *us*! Our reservation number practically blew a circuit. I can't tell you how many limos and cabs and hospitality vans trundled their way over the ice-packed streets from close-by Dallas hotels to get to us, sometimes forming a long, slippery queue down the block. Every dining slot we had was booked solid through Sunday. On the big day, we even extended our hours well past normal closing time to accommodate the post gamers.

I had my head down in the kitchen most of the time and didn't really get a chance to do much star watching, but I can tell you that heavyweights such as Ron Howard, Adam Sandler, Diddy, and Tim Tebow checked in. So did New England Patriots owner Robert Kraft and a bunch of the other NFL team owners. Then, there was rapper/actor Ice Cube, comedian Dennis Miller, film director Michael Bay, and the late politico Rush Limbaugh, who famously tipped one of our servers $2,000 on a $300 tab!

What an honor it was to receive the 2019 True Mavericks Award.

And, of course, that year's Super Bowl halftime performers, The Black Eyed Peas, warmed up for their show with multicourse meals here that week.

We also entertained the multitalented Jamie Fox, radio and television sports-talk host Mike Francesca, Steelers Hall of Famers Terry Bradshaw and Franco Harris, and so many more who came by to see us. Getting with the spirit, a lot of high-profile locals dropped in that week, too.

Unfortunately, many A-listers were upset that, as hard as we tried, we couldn't get them in. Once folks got in and tasted our food, they wanted to book again before they left town—and the next time they came to town. Nick & Sam's became the place to be. Word spread and business has never let up. We have since advanced on our own momentum.

This was more than a decade ago, and "the party" shows no signs of stopping. We aren't going anywhere, except into our patrons' Restaurant Hall of Fame.

I may be called C.C. (celebrity chef), but as I said, I never invited the role. The food that our talented and trusty staff puts out at Nick & Sam's is what really makes *me* popular. Requests like "I just *have* to meet the chef" must always be honored, at least in my book. When these first came, I'd sheepishly appear from out of the "scullery" with a nervous smile, maybe pose for a few photos and engage in a little chitchat.

The stars just sort of seemed to take to me, and I took to them. Maybe it's because they saw me as a modest, nose-to-the-grindstone guy who never wants anything from them, much less an autograph. What I really want is their dining satisfaction.

Plus, our staff goes out of their way to protect these folks from the inevitable gawkers and photo bugs, and they really appreciate that. It makes them feel at ease.

Samir cooking at the James Beard House

Early on, I found it astonishing how many well-known people frequented Nick & Sam's. My good friend Dirk Nowitzki, who was kind enough to write the foreword of this book, was among the first to embrace me as more than just a guy in charge of the kitchen. He immediately struck me with his humbleness and politeness and routinely requested that I pop out to see him when I had the chance. Dirk would come in frequently with his German mentor, Holger Geschwindner, and his good pal Steve Nash, who was then Dirk's teammate. They would treat *me* like a celebrity.

Since then, we've routinely done private dinners for people such as Bieber, Selena Gomez, and Diddy. For his private party, Diddy had a big entourage in tow, all donning letter jackets. As mentioned, Bono was here with several compadres in tow. Billy Bob Thornton came in late one night with his own entourage: his band, The Boxmasters, who had played a gig at the nearby House of Blues. We stayed open late for him, as we often do for other movers and shakers. We've also hosted T. Boone Pickens, Rudy Giuliani, Jimmy Kimmel, and Shaq.

After weekend Mavs home games, we usually get five or more players in, oftentimes with the great Luka Dončić, one of our restaurant's biggest champions, leading the attack. (Luka celebrated his memorable twentieth birthday with us.) The Mavs tend to knife into steaks like they're cutting to the basket, but not all of them do that. Dorian Finney-Smith relishes our Kung Pao Lobster while the lovable, 7-foot 4-inch, 290-pound center Boban Marjanovic—now a Houston Rocket—sticks with *sushi*. Lots of it. And when, God forbid, a Mavs player gets laid up, such as when former Maverick guard J. J. Barea ruptured his Achilles tendon a number of years ago, we send meals to their homes.

We also will deliver post-practice and post-game spreads to the Mavs. Teams like the Boston Celtics, Denver Nuggets, and Golden State Warriors have us cater meals as well, especially the Warriors. Steph Curry loves us. So does NBA legend Scottie Pippin.

We get loads of PGA tour golfers in town for the Byron Nelson tourney, such as the brawny Bryson DeChambeau (who played locally at SMU) and

Tony Romo, Cole, Mia, and Samir

Samir with Luka Dončić

Dallas native Jordan Spieth, plus so many of the big-name coaches and national sportscasters.

When Mr. Clooney walked in one night just after *Ocean's Eleven* was released, he was flocked immediately by onlookers until we politely shooed everyone away.

KISS bassist Gene Simmons was spotted in front of the restroom mirror one night with his portable hair kit splayed out over the two sinks. He was lamenting the dampening effect the humid Dallas weather was having on his trademark jet-black doo.

Countless business types such as Tom Davis, who is chairman of Dean Foods and CEO of The Concorde Group, and Nate Paul, CEO of World Class Capital Group, are regulars, as is the ultimate Dallas mover and shaker, Jerry Jones. You name 'em; we get 'em.

Over the years, we've assembled an extensive collection of about 600 celebrity wine bottles, signed by the larger-than-life set. These are on display, and when the celeb signer returns, we are quick to make sure his or her bottle sits prominently among them. Over the years, most of the Dallas Cowboys and Dallas Mavericks have signed, as have Texas Rangers and Dallas Stars. By the way, these bottles are not for sale or guest access; they're just fun to have around as part of the atmosphere.

One of our managers asked NBA legend Jerry West to sign a 1979 bottle of Opus One Bordeaux when he visited us because that vintage was the first production year for the popular Napa Valley winery—its "rookie card" if you will. Shaq signed another bottle and so did Mr. Bieber.

Michael Keaton came in and graciously signed a bottle just after a widely publicized 9/11 benefit that we had organized, and he added a little Batman logo to boot, dovetailing with his famous movie role at the time.

Needless to say, the celebs dote on our extensive wine list. We have literally hundreds to choose from—from countries ranging from France to Italy to

Samir with Darioush Khaledi, founder of Darioush Winery, Napa, California

Albania—including some very rare vintages. We are one of the few places in the country that sells Champagne Armand de Brignac Brut Gold, a.k.a. "Ace of Spades," by the glass—at a cool $150 "per." A whole bottle will set you back $775. We have a light-up fridge in the bar that displays dozens of Ace of Spades bottles.

Who quaffs these? You'd be surprised. Mavs owner Mark Cuban has been known to tipple an Ace glass or two. So has footballer Johnny Manziel and rapper Chris Brown. When a guest orders Ace of Spades, we roll out a cart, frothing with dry-ice fog, to the table for a little uncorking ceremony.

Others are partial to Screaming Eagle. Some of the rarer bottles—say from 2002 to 2004—can be $1,100 a pop. Another star fave is considerably less pricey. The 2008 Nick & Sam's Cabernet Sauvignon from the Napa Valley's wine epicenter, St. Helena, is less than $100 a bottle.

This would be a fitting time to introduce our sommelier—except we don't have one. What? A five-star fine-dining restaurant without a "somm"?

This bears explaining. We *do* have a dedicated wine person, but he's technically a "wine steward." From the early days, we were adamant that we would not have a real somm, and it didn't take long for me to jump on board. The logic was this: We never want to gouge the guest—or give them the impression they're getting gouged—and sommeliers can do this by pushing certain expensive wines.

Of course, the wines and their strong margins are a crucial part of any fine restaurant staying in the black. However, most wine drinkers, regardless of price point or a diner's personal wealth, still seek value in wine and may look to a fine-dining restaurant's sommelier for objective advice, but somms tend to be actors and storytellers because dining out is entertainment. So, by definition, they are aggressive wine marketers.

And this creates the potential for a conflict of interest or, God forbid, a chance for guests to feel offended should a choice they make be deemed a pairing faux pas. We're not into snobbery here. Besides, everybody carries smartphones today, and guests can easily source reviews and wines' origins and their suggested

retail price, even on rare bottles. The industry margin on wine is around 70 percent, but on rare vintages and other great bottles, it can go as high as three times that, so we want to make sure customers feel comfortable with their choices—and unpressured.

Of course, many diners want to know what wines the chef recommends with certain dishes, so I offer a basic "Chef Samir's Selections" list of fourteen or fifteen excellent wines at reasonable price points that I propose for pairings and personally enjoy. (My wife and I travel to California Wine

Samir and Lori in Napa Valley, California

Country a few times annually for both fun and a little intel.) Ultimately, however, the guest should be the real curator.

Okay, you will remember that actor Michael Keaton did us a favor by custom signing a wine bottle with a Batman logo. Little did we know that he would call on us to return the favor—and in a big way.

Keaton and a movie crew were filming the movie *White Noise* in New Orleans in the summer of 2005, but when Hurricane Katrina menaced, they had to hastily flee to Dallas for safe harbor. Keaton and team needed a place to temporarily stow rigging, costumes, cameras, and other stuff—and pronto. So, he called the lone Dallas number on his phone to see if any Nick & Sam's folks had any ideas. One of our guys volunteered his own garage and home! So, for six weeks, there sat *White Noise*'s equipment and clothes. Nick & Sam's at your service, Michael!

Danilo Di Nardo, Taff Bakali, Samir, and Brad Williams at a Mavericks game

I watch the cooking shows on Food Network, Travel Channel, Netflix, and elsewhere and have my own select list of "C.C.s." Some aren't exactly household names.

The Netflix documentary *Tale of Two Kitchens* was especially interesting to me because it details how one owner/chef, Gabriela Cámara, who is famous for her Contramar restaurant in Mexico City, opened a sister restaurant in the US without losing the founding culture of the original. The new one is called Cala and is in San Francisco. It opened not so much with a similar menu but with a similar employee culture. Culture is universal, and it's so important to the longevity of restaurants, especially ours.

One of my favorite rags-to-riches heroes is Chef Martin Ruiz Salvador of Nova Scotia, who began his career as a dishwasher. In everything he does, like in his Fleur de Sel and Beach Pea Kitchen concepts and more recently his Bar Salvador and Half Shell restaurants, he creates memorable experiences for all his guests, such as nine-course tasting menus and personable interaction. His restaurant culture features all of his crew members playing key roles in delivering great experiences in addition to great food. That's our overriding philosophy at Nick & Sam's as well.

Then, there's the iconic Charlie Trotter, who was never afraid to stray outside established culinary lines at his namesake Chicago eatery. I would have loved to have met and cooked for him, but alas, he unexpectedly died too young—at age 54—in 2013.

Of course, I've admired Gordon Ramsey ever since watching his ground-breaking *Hell's Kitchen* show. He came across as a real mess on the show, but a lot of that was just theatrics. It turns out that he is a really great guy. I also like Michael Symon (he does amazing things with meat) and Michael Mina, Rachel Ray, Paula Deen (a Nick & Sam's patron), and so many others.

I was also fascinated with the late Anthony Bourdain. I ran into him at a Los Angeles restaurant once, and we talked for a long time. Anthony was one of the smartest men I ever met, which is something he clearly projected on his Food Network, Travel Channel, and CNN series. He immediately impressed me with his humanity and his honesty. I respect those qualities in a person and try my best to emulate them.

This ongoing glamorization of celebrity chefs of late has been an absolute boon for the restaurant industry. Chefs are revered now and become point people for their restaurants and personal brands. That hasn't always been the case. All the chef publicity has created more exciting concepts and distinctive restaurant destinations. Another positive is that an increasing number of young people now aspire to be chefs, so we're seeing a lot of fresh industry talent emerge.

We truly have to give credit to rock star–type chefs like Ramsey, Jacques Pépin, and Emeril Lagasse. They've worked extremely hard for their fame and deserve every penny they've made. They've helped make chefs into heroes.

We must also give credit to the original celebrity chef, the inimitable Ms. Child, who got it all started on PBS in the 1960s. Her current PBS show, *Dishing with Julia Child*, features old interviews with her and modern-day takes from celebrity chefs on the recipes and philosophies that helped her show a nation how to cook well, dine well, and drink well.

CHAPTER 4

Honor of a Lifetime: Cooking at the James Beard House

I t's always sweet to be recognized. During my fledgling Nick & Sam's days, I was on cloud nine when I walked away with the American Institute of Wine and Food's prestigious "Upcoming Chef Award" in 2000. I've since been decorated with honors small and great, ranging from firsts in a "Best Caesar Salad Competition," the "Best Food/Wine Matched Menu in Dallas" contest, and so on. These don't include the dozens of awards that Nick & Sam's has garnered, including the prestigious international "Five Star Diamond Award."

However, the highest accolade I ever received and probably ever will receive was an invitation to cook at the esteemed James Beard House in Manhattan, a humble Greenwich Village brownstone that the *New York Times* called the "Vatican of the American food world."

Known as the "Dean of American Cookery," the jovial Mr. Beard was a fabulous chef and a magnanimous man, known for his teachings, cooking lessons, and

Samir in his happy place, the kitchen!

enthusiastic parties with fellow chefs, students, cookbook authors, and colorful guests. Besides his role as instructor par excellence, he authored such bestsellers as *American Cookery*, *The James Beard Cookbook*, and *Beard on Bread* and was an essayist, restaurant consultant, and general emissary for our industry.

Since 1986, chefs have been invited by the James Beard Foundation to "perform" there—that is, cook for a houseful of foundation members and prominent foodies—oftentimes through references from influential industry people.

James Beard House Dinner Team: John Kleifgen, Salvador (Chava) Ordaz, James Beard volunteer (red cap), Giullina Turner, James Beard volunteer (white cap), and Jaime Ramirez

After I unsuccessfully inquired about appearing, I learned through the grapevine that steakhouse chefs were flat-out not getting invited. Period. Whether this was due to a long-held assumption that steakhouse chefs lack skills and finesse in the subtleties of fine cuisine (a notion I disprove every night with the diverse Nick & Sam's menu) I can't be sure, but I persisted and finally got the nod.

But, oh, man, I thought, the pressure is on now. I'd be taking my place at a kitchen shrine, where such stars as Wolfgang Puck, who cooked the inaugural Beard House dinner, Emeril Lagasse, Daniel Boulud, Nobu Matsuhisa, Jacques Pépin, Anthony Bourdain, Marcus Samuelsson, and Charlie Trotter had worked their magic.

To prepare, I was asked to create a complete event proposal, including menus, wines, and preparation details, and send it off to the Beard folks well in advance. I obsessed over the dinner program for weeks, realizing why "be careful what you wish for" was so often muttered by professionals stretching themselves to meet high expectations. While this honor was a great privilege, it also called for a hell of a lot of hard work. What is the "right menu" for this, I wondered? What should I cook and what should I *not* cook? How venturesome can I get? What staff should I take? Where can I do my prep work? And what if, God forbid, I screw up? These questions kept me awake nights.

I've routinely helped prepare 1,000-plus meals per day during my days at Sfuzzi and Nick & Sam's and put together meals for thousands more at a time with charity groups, cooking demos, and so forth. But, to me, the James Beard House, which seats a modest 55, was the biggest stage I would ever find myself on.

While I am normally cool and collected, I was a huge bundle of nerves as I organized this thing. As irony would have it, my appearance at the Beard House would mark yet another connection with the *grande dame* of cooking, Julia Child, who had graciously encouraged me back in the 1980s to hone my craft at the Culinary Institute of America—the best advice I ever received.

After James' death in January of 1985, Julia pressed the industry to honor the man's legacy. Speaking at the International Association of Culinary Professionals conference a few months after his passing, she said that our profession "needs such a place as the Beard House in New York, where we can meet and commune and dine and celebrate, and where we can honor our generous patron saint, James A. Beard."

Stepping up to meet Julia's challenge was her dear friend Peter Kump, a former Beard protégé, who would later found New York City's Institute of Culinary Education. Peter and a consortium of chefs and well-to-do foodies bought the house collectively, and the Beard Foundation was born. Its stated mission is to celebrate, honor, and nurture chefs and other industry stars who help make America's food culture more delicious, diverse, and sustainable for everyone.

After much conjecture, I finally decided on my meal's theme: "Swanky Chophouse." I'll quote the foundation's summary on the dinner invitations: The meal was to be "a glamorous night of prime cuts, caviar, truffles, and more—all inflected with flavors from Chef Samir Dhurandhar's Indian heritage." The gauntlet, as they say, had been cast. People would come expecting a supercharged East-meets-West gastronomic sort of affair, and I had better deliver that with gusto, I thought.

Always having my back, Phil gave me the unconditional thumbs-up to take a talented entourage with me to the Apple, including chef John Kleifgen, manager Brian Knoy (who became G.M. of Nick & Sam's Grill in Park Cities), two sous chefs, two cooks, and even some servers. The New York Institute of Culinary Education would provide me extra staff.

During my flight to the East Coast in the second week of March 2016, I reflected on my decision to depart the Manhattan restaurant scene some seventeen years earlier, recalling my lengthy but fortuitous drive to Dallas in a beater of a car, clinging to a nearly empty wallet, a product of the city's sky-high living expenses. Now, I was returning to the scene as an established chef and favored son of sorts, set to "star" in the city's premiere culinary show with a supporting cast in tow.

For our five-day stay, we boarded at a quaint hotel only a few hundred paces away from the Beard House and even carved out a little time to enjoy the city. For me, that included happy reunions with some of my old restaurant chums at their various establishments. In the East Village, I indulged myself for the first time in succulent Blue Ribbon Chicken, a new eatery that my New York friends just raved about. It's still the absolute best fried chicken I've ever tasted.

As the Beard event neared, I grew increasingly nervous. I don't think I slept a wink the two nights prior. Thank God, my prep space issue was resolved by none other than my old Sfuzzi boss and mentor, Richard Pietromonico, who came up big, giving me the run of one of his commercial kitchens to perform my critical day-before prep work. That was a saving grace that would help me serve a timely, unrushed dinner on the night of the big show on Saturday, March 12.

When we got to the Beard House at 167 West 12th Street, I found the exterior to be unassuming, not unlike the other brownstones in this Chelsea neighborhood. But the charming inside was chock-full of memorabilia from Beard's extraordinary and playful life and projected a warm and happy vibe that seemed to reflect the spirit of the giant of a man who had resided there. Among other revelations, I came to learn of Beard's long history of giving back, including his cofounding of the Citymeals-on-Wheels program, which continues to help feed New York City's homebound elderly today.

When we got into the compact kitchen, I felt a little intimidated, standing on a "stage" that was so central to the grand food culture of this amazing city and the entire culinary world for that matter. It was a surreal, almost out-of-body experience. Here I was, about to prove my mettle in front of a gourmet-minded Manhattan crowd on a culinary stage that was akin to a musician's first eye-opening performance at Carnegie Hall. One thing was sure: I had better be damned good!

Phil Romano would attend, along with my past employers and even several regulars from Dallas, in addition to the Beard Foundation folks and its members. Most would surely be rooting for my success, but a few, I suspect, were thinking I might fall flat on my face in the big city. As if! Pressure has always made me rise to a new level.

There was no time for stage fright as I took charge and got in the zone pretty quickly. All of my worry, preparation, and sweat equity paid off; we served well and on time. As excited guests milled around what had been James Beard's beloved patio garden, my trusty group of helpers passed around our distinctive hors d'oeuvres. We offered Crab Cake Poppers with Tomato Preserves, Chicken Liver Crostini with Port Jelly, Apple Fennel Slaw, Papadam with Spiced Eggplant and Gorgonzola, and Crispy Oyster Sliders with Barbecued Beef Bacon. The latter, in particular, disappeared like a dream. For patio aperitifs we served Armand de Brignac's iconic—and expensive—"Ace of Spades" Brut. If *this* doesn't get them in the mood, I don't know what will, I thought.

Then came the dinner seating and the rest of our grandiose multicourse Swanky Chophouse feast. We doled out a sumptuous surf-and-turf duo of Allen Brothers Prime Filet and Blue Fin Toro with Caviar, Truffles, and Pickled Fresno Chiles and a Little Gem Caesar Salad with Crisp Eggs and Bottarga. Then came our crowd-pleasing Ohmi Beef Tenderloin with Cipollini, Oxtail Croquettes and King Crab Oscar, Australian Wagyu Short Rib Cannelloni with Parmigiano-Reggiano Fonduta, and one of my native favorites, Chilean Sea Bass with Tikka

Masala Sauce, Salted Cod Brandade, Mustard Greens, and Chili Onions—certainly not your run-of-the-mill Saturday-night dinner.

We paired courses with American wines from California, Washington, and Oregon and then offered a robust Gingersnap Cappuccino with Candied Pecans, Cappuccino Foam, and Chocolate Miso Brûlée after the meal. Voila!

New Yorkers can be fickle, but our diverse cast of guests raved. Their compliments seemed genuine and uncontrived, beyond just "polite." I was pretty sure, at this point, that the Beard Foundation folks were glad they took a chance on this slightly charred Indian steakhouse cook and Dallasite. I shyly basked in everyone's approval—not really my strong suit—or at least as much as my inborn humility would allow. The "performance" was nearly over, and I took my bow. Relieved, I began taking deep breaths, finally chilling out a bit once the post-dinner drinks were downed and the tables cleared.

Phew. When did I feel completely at ease? Only when I returned to my hotel room, took my shoes off, and put my feet up, clutching a tall Dewars-and-soda and then another. I lapsed into a tired state of satisfaction and smiled contentedly, realizing the Beard House dinner had been one of the most heartwarming—and yes, unnerving—experiences of my life. Here's to you, James Beard, and all the chefs you inspired and motivated. That night, I lapsed into a deep and restful sleep for the first night in a very long time.

As I look back, preparation had won the day but so had practice. As a prelude to the big dinner, we had hosted a trial run at Nick & Sam's a few weeks earlier, inviting all of our regulars. Not only were they ecstatic with their "sneak peek," but also, before the plates were cleared, some of them had decided that they would fly out to New York for the main event redux. Some even hired me to recreate the menu for private parties at their homes.

My Beard House appearance generated a lot of press. FOX 4's *Good Day* invited me on camera to prepare something off that menu. I chose the Crab

FOX 4's *Good Day* crew being treated to Samir's cooking

Cakes with Preserves. *D Magazine* did a big spread on all my Beard dinner offerings, and local and regional newspapers also made note of the exclusive event.

For the longest time, I was glowing. About a month after the event, we got at it again, preparing a six-course gourmet feast at Nick & Sam's, based on what I served at the New York event. There were no complaints!

My advice for aspiring chefs who wish to "perform" at the Beard House some day: Start from the bottom but never lose sight of the top. Do your time, put in the hard work, rise above and beyond, and strive to learn and to get better every single day! It's hard to go wrong when you're exceeding expectations. If a naive kid fresh from India, who at first couldn't identify half of the American restaurant ingredients at culinary school, can rise to the Beard stage, so can any conscientious chef with a little imagination and a *lot* of dedication and determination.

To me, a professional honor is not just something that I, or we at Nick & Sam's, win or receive. Rather, some of the most meaningful honors come through our ability to help out people in the community.

I've been very fortunate to have so much: a great job, great family, and great life. There isn't a day that goes by that I don't recognize and appreciate how blessed I am. I was *very* fortunate to be on the receiving end of good breaks in my career just when I needed them. Sfuzzi executive chef Richard Pietromonico took a chance on a foreign kid fresh out of culinary school who didn't even have legal status to work in the US. His kindness and patience helped give me a much-needed pathway to success and, ultimately, citizenship. Phil Romano also took a big chance on me, a broke Indian chef, when he hired me in the late 1990s to head the kitchen of his signature steakhouse creation.

Still, not everybody catches a break when they most need it. So, when I see people hurting, I ask myself what I can do to give back. Even when I'm stopped at a traffic light and a street person approaches my car for a handout, I give him or her something. Who am I to say what that money is going to be used for, or for that matter, to judge that person? Most of the folks out there have had a rough road and so many are mentally ill. At least, I know I have in some small way helped them survive.

During the early—and certainly the worst—months of the COVID-19 pandemic, it was clear that a ton of people were suffering and that scores of dedicated people were risking their lives daily to take care of them. It was heart-breaking to watch this play out. So, I wondered, What could I do? The answer became clear: feed the hundreds of heroes in our community who were tending to the gravely ill. But how?

When COVID was really taking hold, some of our own workers got sick, sadly, so we took a break and shut down the dining room for a while. We were only offering to-go orders.

A number of our loyal customers, who came in during this time to grab what was probably the best "takeout" in DFW, wanted to be sure that our workers were taken care of while the dining room was closed. So, they "tipped" generous sums, often saying something to the effect of: "Hey, give this to your staff." Many gave several hundred dollars. Some even more.

We love and respect all of our employees, so, yes, we were making absolutely sure they were being taken care of during this very challenging period. We partners suspended our own pay during this time to help make that happen; it was an easy decision to make.

But there was still the question of what to do with all the thousands of dollars we got in donated money. We quickly reached a consensus to give a

DARS (Division for Blind Services) Program participants cook with Samir.

much-needed break to all the nurses, EMTs, doctors, and other caregivers at area hospitals, who were putting their lives on the line, by delivering to them a mini culinary vacation, just to momentarily remove them from their rigorous COVID-fighting grind.

So, we stocked up on product, called in a crew, and cranked up a kitchen assembly line early one April morning in 2020. Before we knew it, we had assembled hundreds of meals. We loaded up the Nick & Sam's catering van and some other vehicles to deliver a little culinary healing to the folks at four hospitals who have done a lot for us: Baylor Medical Center, UT Southwestern, Parkland, and Medical City. These meals were a welcome relief from the standard hospital fare. Caregivers dined on filet mignon, Ora King salmon, penne ala vodka, salad, and cheesecake.

It was just one small way of saying thanks to those who saved and served so many ailing people during the pandemic. *They* were the true celebrities—community heroes all. We fed more than 2,000 people that day, I'm proud to say, plus a couple hundred more at Methodist Richardson Medical Center days after that. While the recipients thanked us profusely, the real thanks go to them and those generous Nick & Sam's customers whose donations made it all possible. It's always heartwarming to see how far a little goodwill can go.

Over the years, it's been rewarding to work with so many charities, especially those involving kids. Top among them is Hunger Busters, the charity that Phil founded in 1999, just around the time Nick & Sam's was getting going. It now provides a much-needed third daily meal to the hundreds of food-insecure kids in the Dallas Independent School District. Over the years, we've stepped up to "feed the need" for them with food, labor, and fundraising—whatever it takes.

We assist organizations such as the March of Dimes, the Texas Neurofibromatosis Foundation, and the Department of Assistive and Rehabilitative Services (DARS), which benefits children with developmental

Texas Neurofibromatosis Foundation host child and Samir

Mavs Christmas Event: Grayson, Mia, Samir, Dirk, and Cole

delays, among many, many other great organizations. It's the kind of work that doesn't really *seem* like work. Plus, it always makes me thankful for my own family's copious blessings.

Seeing those smiles on the kids' faces always makes my day—my week. The fortunate members of our society take far too many things for granted and need to pause occasionally for perspective.

One particularly satisfying thing I'm privileged to do is to help teach young blind people to cook. During local radio station KRLD's annual Restaurant Week, I joined chefs throughout Dallas to cook meals for a big benefit for the North Texas Food Bank and Lena Pope Home (a child-development organization), waking well before sunup one morning to prepare hundreds of dinners—Beef Tenderloin with Wild Mushrooms and Blue-Corn Crusted Salmon with all the extras—for the evening benefit.

I needed to get this little labor of love out of the way early that day because I had booked a big noon engagement: working with blind students through the

Blind Services division of the Texas Department of Assistive and Rehabilitative Services to familiarize them with the intricacies of preparing meals. In all, seventeen students took part, all legally blind and all donning chef hats for the occasion.

Sure, there were a few challenges—sharp knives, for example, as well as the inevitable onion teardrops and the delicate balancing act of carting around full cookware and glassware. So, caution was important to me and the other area chefs who turned out to help. But we all watched in amazement as the highly tuned senses of these budding, instinctive junior chefs segued into a form of "sight" that few seeing people could fathom.

It was especially rewarding to watch the kids dine on a feast that they had prepared. It's been my pleasure to do this whenever asked—at least a couple of times a year. How good can a sight-impaired chef be? Legally blind chef Christine Ha was the first blind winner of the *MasterChef* show back in 2012!

We also like to leverage our dining room and gracious friends to help us give back. In silent auctions at the annual Mavs Ball fundraiser gala put on by the Dallas Mavericks over the past three years, fans won "Dinner with Friends" at Nick & Sam's with Luka Dončić and Dirk Nowitzki. One bidder even threw down six figures for the honor! Mavs Ball raises over $1 million annually for kids' services and other very worthy causes, including food for families affected by the COVID crisis.

My right-hand chef, John, and I have done food showcases benefitting the National Kidney Foundation and other organizations. I've done cooking demos at benefits such as Sandlot Children's Charity's "Swinging Fore a Cause" fundraiser and at such varied places as the Dallas Farmers Market, Williams Sonoma, and

Samir sits on the judges panel for the Big Tex Choice Awards during the State Fair of Texas.

the Texas State Fair. (I was a Big Tex Choice Awards judge in the 2019 Texas fair, and the winner was Fried Taco Cone. The losers felt heartbreak, but we judges felt mostly heartburn.)

We work with Mark Cuban and the Mavericks on so many other things, including Seats for Soldiers, where Nick & Sam's feeds a four-course meal to a large group of our heroes who arrive here from around the country and then shove off to a Mavs game.

I've participated in innumerable cooking contests, like the North vs. South Celebrity Chef Smackdown, where chefs get a mystery basket of ingredients and have just 45 minutes to create a winning dish. I have sparred with other chefs in the regional Stainless Steel Competition, have been a judge for countless cooking competitions, and regularly participate in media interviews and podcasts throughout the year. I relish these invites as an honor.

We never do charitable things just for PR value, though the media catches up with us from time to time, and that's fine. Sometimes, good deeds can beget good things.

Here's a prime example: We held a Thanksgiving Day benefit way back in 2001 for the widows of firefighters and police officers killed on 9/11. *The Dallas Morning News* talked with us and took some pics, but we only expected a blurb to appear. But there was huge splash in the paper, including a giant photo, on Thanksgiving Eve about the extensive needs of 9/11 survivors. The response at the restaurant was absolutely insane. Nick & Sam's took in more than 700 reservations, and we filled the place all day, allowing us to donate more than $20,000 of the proceeds to the families. That really helped set the table for our early public recognition and success and gave us a much-needed bridge to our next generation of good fortune. Our own families didn't see us much, but it sure was a nice way to give thanks on Thanksgiving Day.

I mention these efforts not to toot our horns but to give other restaurants, chefs, and businesses a few ideas about how they can utilize their people and resources to give back to the community that supports them.

You are only limited by your imagination when it comes to finding ways to give back to your fellow man. So, get crackin'!

CHAPTER 5

Strange Tales from the Kitchen: The Ghosts and the Tenor

As you now know, the forerunner of Nick & Sam's was Lawry's The Prime Rib. But before that, our 65-year-old building at 3008 Maple Avenue was an auxiliary morgue!

In our earlier days of operation, a few of our older guests from our Uptown neighborhood brought in photos to prove this fact, and I saw them. Indeed, it had been an eerie place, utilized by the city of Dallas and the old Parkland Memorial Hospital as a "charnel house" for more than a decade before Lawry's took it over in the 1970s. In other words, there was plenty of cold storage here well before the two restaurants came.

Parkland, by the way, is where a mortally wounded John F. Kennedy was transported in November of 1963 after the infamous downtown assassination. At that time, Parkland sat at the corner of Maple Avenue and Oak Lawn, just over a half mile from our roomy 12,000-square-foot building, which was constructed in 1958. Parkland later moved to a modern new building a little to the north.

But this "run-over" morgue saw plenty of intakes in its heyday. That little bit of history was interesting when I first heard it, but to be honest, I hadn't given it much thought. That is, until I walked in Nick & Sam's early one afternoon and spotted a well-dressed older woman sitting by herself in one of the booths near the kitchen. She turned to watch me walk past her.

Seeing someone sitting in our dining room at this early hour was unusual because we don't serve lunch, and we don't open until 5 p.m. There was no private party or special event scheduled that day. Odd.

The waiting woman wore professional, if a little outmoded, garb. So, I just figured she was here for a job interview. When I strolled in the kitchen and saw that a few of our people had already arrived, I immediately asked, "Was anybody interviewing someone today or meeting someone for any reason? If so, she's out there waiting." They shook their heads no and sort of looked at each other quizzically. "In that case," I wondered aloud, "who is that woman sitting out there?"

So, I backtracked posthaste to the booth. The waiting woman, however, had vanished in the minute or two I was in the kitchen. She was nowhere to be found on the premises. Surely, she had been there, plain as day, hadn't she? Were my eyes deceiving me?

I would soon discover that this was far from the only unexplained event that had occurred around the restaurant since it opened. As I talked with individual staff members, the peculiar stories started coming out.

Several reported they had seen folks opening the door to our storage area at the end of the bar and entering, only to never reemerge. The same went for the bar bathroom. "Guests" walked in and didn't come out. And there was no alternative way to exit from either room. When staffers tried to track down these malingerers, they were, of course, nowhere to be found. Other workers would hear someone talking in the office, knock on the slightly cracked door, and then enter to find no one there.

Some staffers said they had glanced out into the dining room to notice an odd group of people gathered in a booth. But no one had seated them. At next glance, these phantom diners seemed to suddenly disappear, much like the woman I saw.

Busboys regularly report someone or something trying to hold them back when they attempt to maneuver through the busy kitchen with armloads of trays and dishes.

What's more, our bar people reported that magic markers in the bar area just started moving on their own one Sunday. And, no, I don't think our bartenders drink on the job.

I've even heard mysterious voices softly calling out "Samir" when no one else is around. "Who's there?" I always ask. Dead silence.

Before a wine wall was constructed to form a hallway that leads to our main restroom just prior to our opening, several different staff members independently reported glancing into the then-doorless restrooms from the dining room, only to see a litany of smiley faces plastered all over the walls. But upon closer inspection, there was nary a wall smile to be found.

My own family, having experienced some peculiar movements and object displacements over the years after I came home from work, suspect that I'm taking these things home with me at night. While it's good to have friends over, I generally prefer to entertain living guests!

What do I think? Whenever I hear the old saying, "if these walls could talk," I wonder if these walls actually *can* talk and if our guest ghosts run rampant in the wee hours, hosting soirees and meetings.

Over time, I've come to view these strange occurrences with less and less alarm and more as part of the mystique and history of the place. Perhaps these "ghosts" or "spirits," after what must have seemed an eternity on a cold slab, are just glad to be hanging around Nick & Sam's. After all, we offer them hot grills and ovens, warm conversation, and an interesting assortment of people to prank, and certainly a measurable step-up in decor.

One thing is abundantly clear: They don't tip well.

I recall yet another strange entity entering my kitchen, this time at the Manhattan Sfuzzi one afternoon during my exec chef stint there. It wasn't a ghost, but, nevertheless, a little startling, as some feisty Sicilians can be.

Late one morning, just as I arrived for duty, I was informed that we would be closing to the general public that night to accommodate a dinner party for an extraordinary V.I.P. guest of grand international stature.

That description was no exaggeration. As it turned out, the most beloved Italian operatic tenor in the world, the larger-than-life Luciano Pavarotti, would soon be taking over the place for a party. Pavarotti, who was living in Manhattan at the time, clearly had a grand appetite for life, and a big part of that was his zest for fine New York food, particularly Italian. We would be performing for *him* that night.

And we'd be getting a little unsolicited help. That afternoon, Pavarotti's personal Italian-American chef strode in the door. He skipped the pleasantries and marched straight back to our kitchen. There, he asked me—or should I say "demanded"—to taste the tomato sauce. He spooned a sample, sipped it, swished it around in his mouth, and then winced. He proceeded to denounce it as little more than trash, even going so far as to compare it to "store-bought."

The Sicilian sure pissed off some people with this abrasive grand entrance, including me. He then made us an offer that we literally couldn't refuse. *He* would be taking the "pressure off of us" by making the sauce tonight in a traditional manner that Pavarotti had grown accustomed, using *sabato trippa,* or a beef tripe foundation, for his Tripe alla Romana specialty. Tripe, if you don't know, is the first and second stomach of a cow. It was quite apparent that this tripe sauce thing was going to happen whether we liked it or not.

As if to apologize for his rudeness, the Sicilian said he would be glad to teach me and the other food preparers how to create it. One of his secrets, besides the tripe, was to deftly combine San Marzano plum tomatoes, which are longer, thinner, and more flavorful than standard plum tomatoes, with fresh regular hand-picked tomatoes.

But before he could do that, he startled us again. Without explanation, he started hammering out an empty clean No. 10 commercial-sized can, which was roughly 7 inches tall and 6 inches wide. He eventually flattened the thing completely, all the time babbling about "heat distribution." Some of our folks hurried back to the kitchen from the dining room floor to see what the clamor was, only to find an outsider wailing on a metal can with a hammer.

Finally, the Sicilian rested this almost perfectly flattened commercial can atop our biggest burner, finally explaining that it would facilitate an even distribution of both the heat and sauce bubbles to create a perfect consistency that would be most pleasing to the fickle Pavarotti. The chef proceeded to cook the sauce very slowly over low heat, judiciously dropping in small strips of tripe from time to time, which he had also personally precooked.

As a bonus, the chef said, he would show us all how to cook a fritter—another Pavarotti favorite—without turning it. "A fritter made right will flip on its own," he assured us. We looked at each other with skepticism.

But to our amazement, flop! There it went. None of us could master the trick nor did we feel a need to fritter away any more of our valuable time doing so if you'll pardon the pun. The clock was ticking. I could almost envision the great Pavarotti starting to primp for his big night at Sfuzzi, and there was still a lot of prep to do.

Sure, it wasn't exactly *O Sole Mio* in our kitchen that night, but we got this thing done collectively and quite well, at least in my humble opinion. The great tenor didn't sing for his supper that night or serenade us at all.

But he did sing, at least figuratively, the praises of his perfectly rich, tripe-y Sicilian sauce, the self-turning fritters, our vibrant venue, and Sfuzzi's food and service contributions. It was a huge win for the big tenor, the organizers, and Sfuzzi. And, oh, yeah, for our Sicilian chef friend as well, who, like Nick & Sam's multiple ghosts, finally disappeared into the night.

(Opposite) Jose Gamboa making his magic

CHAPTER 6

Dishing with Samir: A Dash of Savvy, a Pinch of Wisdom, and Those Golden Rules

I n this rich serving of Q & A and professional tips, our resident celeb chef Samir spills the beans about his favorite dishes, most hated foodstuffs, preferred aperitifs, and rare spats with bosses, while divulging his happy place.

Q **You were the man in charge of the Nick & Sam's kitchen from the get-go on opening night 1999. That seems like a lot of pressure. Did you have anyone to help guide you those first few months?**

SAMIR: Yes, lucky for me. We brought in Nick Badovinus, who had a lot of talent and experience, as our opening executive sous chef, and he really pushed me to be a better chef. He has a passion for cooking that I had never seen anywhere else, and he helped me realize that I could cook pretty much anything—and well. He was a huge influence.

Q How do you keep things interesting and exciting for your guests who have already dined with you dozens of times?

SAMIR: We have regulars who've literally visited us *hundreds* of times. Some join us two or three times a week. So, we have to keep things extraordinary for them. I often say that people go to a restaurant the first time for the food and go the second time for the service. If you give them both at 100 percent every time, you have a guest who will come back again and again. Sure, other steakhouses may have some of the same meats as we do, but we provide the flair and the theatrics surrounding them: the way the meat is plated, the swarm of service on all sides of the table, the grand piano playing in the back room, the bustle of the dining room—all of that is stimulating and a part of the show. Then, there are things that nobody around town does, like the big cotton candy we serve and the seven-layer cakes topped with lit sparklers going out to the tables.

You also have to give guests something unique all the time. It's true that it's never wise to mess with your guests' favorites, but you still need to keep the menu fresh, so we're always considering potential new menu items to stay ahead of the times. If our menu doesn't change, customers will respond by reducing their visits. It's why our

Samir, Michael Bublé, and Lori

restaurant is filled to the brim every night. A lot of restaurants stay stagnant, and their clientele slowly disappears.

Q How do you gauge what guests would like to see on the menu?

SAMIR: That's the second part of the equation. Our managers and other staff are in constant conversation with our guests about this very thing. We ask our people on the floor to casually broach that topic at least two or three times per night with different guests throughout the restaurant. For our part, we are constantly experimenting to create something new and unconventional and special. That led to our authentic Japanese Wagyu beef offerings, which are as diverse and thorough as at any restaurant in the US, and our wide variety of sushi. Nothing like this was on our menu when we opened. But it was something we knew our diners would take to, in part because we asked them first.

Pro Tip

There is one consistent way to serve the best meat: Buy the best in the land. We firmly believe that Allen Brothers of Chicago fits the bill. Their meat arrives already expertly aged for twenty-eight days. That's a great start. But when we get it, we wet-age the meat—that is, vacuum-seal it—for fourteen more days to let the enzymes in the juices finish breaking down the collagen fibrils. This optimizes tenderness. A lot of folks think you must marinate, but if you use the highest quality beef, there's no need. I just use pepper and salt for seasoning.

Samir, Cole, Mia, Isabella Taylor, and Lori at Allen Brothers in Chicago

Q Have you ever thrown down your apron, grabbed your knives, and charged out the door in a huff at any point in your career, like so many chefs have?

SAMIR: Ha! No, but I did get shown the door once. In my younger and inexperienced—okay, my hothead—days, a pushy bartender charged into the kitchen, wanting an order of linguini and clams right away, and we were slammed. He kept coming back; his visits were a few minutes apart. He complained to the general manager, who came in and gave me a dirty look as the bartender loomed nearby. By then, I had plated the linguini in question and yelled, "Here it is." And I just flung the whole thing at them. Order up! I got suspended for a week and probably deserved it. Sometimes, you have to learn to just walk away from a situation. To this day, though, I do impress upon my wait staff that they must not be afraid to go to the chef if a guest sends something back. We don't even serve linguini here anyway, so everybody is safe! (Laughs)

Q Have you gotten crossways with legendary Nick & Sam's founder/partner Phil Romano?

SAMIR: In twenty-four years, Phil has only gotten pissed at me once. I had sprayed all the stainless steel in the kitchen with a cleaning solution, but I got distracted and didn't get around to cleaning and rinsing it before Phil came in. So, there it was, sitting there, all crusty and dirty looking. He walked in, saw that mess, and yelled, "Samir, this place is filthy. I couldn't even bring a cow in here!" Holy cow!

Pro Tip

Clean as you go! We've all glanced into commercial kitchens, only to see remnants of foodstuffs lying around, walls caked with spatters, and dirty cookware piling up. This projects a negative image in the eyes of diners, workers, and inspectors.

So, it's important to clean on the fly. Aside from preventing cross-contamination and bacteria spread, this approach also frees up valuable workspace and makes for a far more manageable cleanup at night's end. This is a good policy at home, too.

Q **Do you hire your staffers mostly for a single role, or do you cross-train them?**

SAMIR: A little bit of both. We are in the business of educating our people. So, as a rule, we cross-train people for various posts until we find a place where they are most comfortable. For our new cooks, we have them working with spices they've never used before and dishes they've never cooked before and, in general, doing something different every day. We'll throw them a curveball and say something like, "Okay, today, you will learn the perfect way to poach fish." But we also have people who've chosen to remain in the same position, not because they can't fit in elsewhere, but because they love what they do and are so good at it that they prefer to remain there.

Q **What about you? Can you fill in where needed?**

SAMIR: Absolutely. That's part of being a team. I can take over any job, except don't put me on the broiler and grill station. Phew! Those guys are so amazing, working over that intense heat all night, and they are so consistent. They can do 800 meals a night and *maybe* get two sent back.

Pro Tip

We've all heard the expression "the greatest thing since sliced bread." While it may be hard to improve on the nearly 100-year-old innovation, what about enhancing the simple act of slicing bread? When I was breaking into the trade, my old Sfuzzi boss, Richard Pietromonico, actually taught me a better way to slice bread after watching me hack my way through a freshly made loaf. Richard held up a very sharp serrated knife and said, "Samir, instead of you doing all the work, let the teeth of the knife do the work." Focusing on the serration and using just his fingers to apply pressure, he effortlessly sliced consistent-sized pieces in quick, clean motions, while applying as little downward pressure as possible. It was almost as if Richard was slicing warm butter.

Q What do you look for in job applicants?

SAMIR: First, I will ask them why they want to work at Nick & Sam's. After all, if it's just for a paycheck, they can get that anywhere. We are seeking a specific, motivated type of individual. I ask them what they are going to give to make the people around them successful. I look for drive and passion—people who are eager to give me all they've got, whether they know much about the business or not. I will hire those people any day over an experienced person whose motivations and background are questionable. I want someone who has an appetite to get better every day.

Samir with the famous Benny of Nick & Sam's

Q With so many long-term employees, do you really have to interview much?

SAMIR: I always try to interview people whether we need someone or not. You never know who's going to walk in the door. Take my chef, John Kleifgen. He walked in cold one Wednesday afternoon, asking about a position, and I could tell he had that something we were looking for. He has been with me more than six years now. I even cooked for his wedding! People like him make my life a lot easier and the restaurant a lot better. Like a great sports team, you can never close your eyes to promising new prospects.

Pro Tip

Here's a garlic "hack." At Nick & Sam's, we plunge our garlic cloves in hot water for about a half hour during prep time. This makes that slightly gooey layer between the skin and the clove dissipate and causes the peels to swell. This either forces the skin off entirely or makes it very easy to remove it with your fingers.

Q Are there any special "golden rules" you have for your servers to ensure great service?

SAMIR: Number one: Never say no to a guest; we are not in the business of saying no. You can always find a way of granting any request. Number two: Never lie to a guest about anything; don't cover for yourself or anybody else because we all are accountable to the guest. Number three: Let us know what is going on at your table. If it's a birthday or celebration, my duty is to help create the best one ever for them. If there is a problem, we want to know about it right away. We are here to create memories. And yes, this requires extra effort. People who don't try, don't work here long.

Q How do you feel about food critics?

SAMIR: As a young chef in New York, I hated them. We chefs work long hours, and it's simple human nature that if you are really devoted to something, it's hard when someone goes negative, especially in public. At first, I felt like they were all gunning for me. But the more I thought about it, I saw that some of their criticism could be a wake-up call and an opportunity for improvement, because I truly hate for any guests to have a less than exemplary experience. So, we would find ways to make sure that we got better. Still, reviews are subjective and just one person's opinion.

Pro Tip

I've won many cooking competitions, including the salad specialty. The judges tend to "hail" my Caesar salads. Mine, you see, are a little different and here's how: Most people toss their Caesar dressing in the salad, where it tends to coat the tongue and linger well after you finish it, affecting the taste of the next course. To mitigate this, I add a little heavy cream, treating the dressing more like a sauce. I also make absolutely sure it coats the lettuce leaves evenly. This way, you still get all the flavor, but your taste buds won't be overwhelmed for the rest of the meal.

Q What makes the Dallas culinary scene unique from other markets?

SAMIR: I think it's the versatility of the restaurant guests coming to this city from all over the globe. Being centrally located in the US in a region with a huge diversity of industry, Dallas gets all types. It's really on the brink of being recognized as a major food town if it isn't already. The increasing amount of investment here and the population growth and great new restaurants are helping. Visitors, to some degree, still see Dallas as only a meat-and-potatoes town, but they're pleasantly surprised when they find we're so much more. In my opinion, Dallas has already evolved into a gastronomic epicenter.

Q When it's time to kick back, what's your favorite drink?

SAMIR: I love all kinds of wine, but when it comes to cocktails, I like the simplicity of Dewars and soda. But I am also a sucker for a really spicy Bloody Mary with extra jalapeño-stuffed olives!

Q What's your favorite kitchen tool or gadget?

SAMIR: It's my Japanese slicer, or "smart cleaver," which is like five different knives. You can play around with it and make unique strings of vegetables and other creative treatments. It's also really handy with proteins like sushi, octopus, and short ribs, to name only a few. I also can't live without my Vitamix. It's the ultimate blender.

Q If you hadn't become a chef, what would you have been?

SAMIR: Truly, I can't imagine being anything else. Maybe a teacher or a food critic . . . but with a huge home kitchen.

Q Out of all those ingredients you work with, do you find any particular one distasteful?

SAMIR: Yes, I must confess. It's avocados! I just never liked them. But I realize most of our guests like avocados, and I use them to make sauces and relishes. I just have one of our avocado fans on the staff do the taste-testing. "Please," I implore them.

Pro Tip

Add some vitamin D to green sauces. It makes (and keeps) sauces a brighter green. Diners can always use a little extra mood-enhancing vitamin D in their diets, especially in winter when they get little sun.

Q You've used your skills at a steakhouse for twenty-four years, but do you ever long to cook "off the menu" there with some of your favorite Indian dishes or other international fare that the restaurant doesn't serve?

SAMIR: I already do it. One Sunday a month, we hold "eat-till-you're-full" family dinners in a party room with different international themes. We call these "Sunday Suppers." They only seat seventy-five and always sell out fast. For me and others in the kitchen, these are more about our chefs having fun and demonstrating their flexibility than making money for Nick & Sam's. We skip around from French food one week to Italian the next to Mediterranean and so on. I love a good challenge, and I like to play with ingredients that I rarely work with. That sort of thing makes me a better chef. Sometimes, we showcase specialties from my native India. It's fun to hear raves about some of my Indian favorites, like Dhaka-Style Crisp Halibut with Red Chiles and Sesame Seeds or Lobster Kebabs with Mint and Basil.

Pro Tip

Don't mess with your people's money! Our workers and their families depend on me and all of their scheduled hours for their paychecks. So, honor their schedules! Of course, unlike so many corporately owned chain restaurants, we aren't pressed to send people home early to save a few bucks. If we're a little overstaffed on occasion, in effect, we managers just say, "Let's just keep them on; they need to get paid." This lets me be a better manager, a better chef, and a better person, because I am able to make things good for all of my great kitchen staffers, and they stick with me as a result and step up to perform when things get crazy. Their happiness is of the utmost importance because they make me look good every day.

Samir with live lobsters

Q Do you have a signature dish at Nick & Sam's?

SAMIR: My favorite creation here is the Kung Pao Lobster. I took the Texanized chicken-fried lobster treatment and added a spicy Asian twist (my tip on this dish follows). It's a customer favorite and a personal one for me, too.

Q Foodies always want to know what a celebrity chef cooks at home. Enlighten us a little please.

SAMIR: I cook a little bit of everything. But Indian food is probably my favorite. I cook a mean curry, but I guess Indian kabobs are my ideal comfort food. I have a tandoor oven in the backyard for that very reason. Our pantry is full of the same ingredients my mom used. My wife has become quite the accomplished Indian-food chef as well.

Q What are your favorite spices at home and at work?

SAMIR: Ginger! I grew up in India with all those ginger combinations such as ginger-garlic. They are just lovely for sushi and other Japanese food and so much more. Cumin is another. Not only is cumin an essential spice for the Indian curries I make at home, but I also use it for other dishes at the restaurant. It's also very healthy. It's an antioxidant and anti-inflammatory. At home, garam masala is an essential, too. Every Indian kitchen has some version of it, and there are so many versions. Cardamom and clove and coriander are also basics at home and, of course, plenty of dried chilies.

I need to point out that most people who've never traveled to India don't realize that Indian cuisine and spices vary greatly from region to region. In the north, the foods are heavier with a lot of fat and butter and curries. But if you go west toward the Arabian Sea, it's a lot more seafood based. In the south, it is more diverse and more spice based. I discovered some of the best Indian "street food" along the highways at truck stops while on a road trip to visit old friends. "Frankies," a sort of Indian burrito, include ingredients like brains, kidney, chilies, and vinegar and onions smothered in eggs. All the truck stops have slightly different versions of them. Absolutely delicious.

Pro Tip

Throw away kitchen "leftovers"? Why? When there are remnants left over from fresh preparation, there is usually a way to use them. For example, when we cut our meat, we save the bones and then deep freeze them. They are later used to enhance soups and add flavor and nutrition to sauces, fish stock, and other things. Don't waste quality foodstuffs. It's part of working smarter.

Q

Foodies always want to know where the best chefs dine out. Where do you?

SAMIR: When we go out for Indian, a place called India Palace on I-635 in Dallas pretty much offers the same types of food and sauces that my mother made. This is very hard to find anywhere in the states. We also like Maharaja in Plano, north of Dallas. For Chinese dim sum, we love Kirin Court in Richardson. Dim sum is sharing, and there's nothing better than dining with friends and family.

Q

Outside of the DFW area, what are some of your favorite restaurants?

SAMIR: Places that stand out at the top for me are Thomas Keller Ad Hoc in Yountville, California, and a Vietnamese place called The Slanted Door in San Francisco. For steaks, I enjoy STK Steakhouse in Los Angeles, which is very imaginative. One of my all-time favorites, Gotham Bar and Grill in Manhattan, sadly closed permanently due to COVID. I would go in there every time I was in town. I also love the Tao restaurants and anything else that Sam Hazen is behind. He is a great chef and was a mentor of mine during my days at the Culinary Institute of America and later in New York with the Heartland Brewery Restaurant Group.

Q

What made Chef Hazen such a good mentor?

SAMIR: He was very patient with me. At the CIA, we had a class called The Experimental Kitchen, and Sam was the chef instructor. He taught me how to get organized and showed me how to "fix" things as I cooked. For example, if a hollandaise (mix) breaks, you might just think to throw it out and start all over. But he taught us how to fix the broken emulsion. He opened up a whole new way of thinking for me. What makes you a better chef is learning how to manage your mistakes and rectify them. Isn't that true about life too?

Pro Tip

Our Kung Pao Lobster gets raves for both its distinctiveness and zest. Traveled diners call it "one-of-a-kind." What's the secret? First, we import the finest lobsters in the world: West Australian lobster tails. Then, we flash-fry the lobsters and immediately toss them with my custom Kung Pao sweet-and-spicy sauce, using a punch-packing sauce from a proprietary recipe I picked up long ago in New York. Then, we get these little beauts right out to the table for maximum zing. They're usually ordered as hors d'oeuvres, but many diners ask for double servings to create an entrée. Cravedfw.com calls them "divine."

Q You mentioned Chef Hazen, Richard Pietromonico, and, of course, Julia Child, as big personal influences. Do others come to mind?

SAMIR: My partner, Phil Romano, is a big one. He pushes me to be better. He and the managers took the time to show me the business side of the industry and its link to the kitchen and how to take care of everyone who walks through the door. The guest is always royalty.

Q How do you know you are getting the highest quality foodstuffs for your patrons with so many different suppliers showing up at all hours?

SAMIR: For all deliveries, we check every single item at the door. Some of my more eagle-eyed guys do this (I will do it, too), and if we see a delivery is not top level in freshness and appearance, we send it back. Take asparagus, for example. If the stalks aren't firm and the tips aren't closed or they look a little dry or ridged, they're going back. I'd rather do that than take a chance on presenting anything subpar to the guests. People have high expectations when they visit Nick & Sam's, so quality control is extremely important, and it starts with deliveries.

Q What are some of your biggest kitchen-prep challenges?

SAMIR: One thing we do at Nick & Sam's that I think is underappreciated and very hard to do is hand make every single layer of our seven-layer cake. We do about fifty of those (vanilla) cakes a week for birthdays and other celebrations, and each layer is dyed a different color of the rainbow and baked separately. Then, they are hand frosted with butter cream. It is very labor intensive. We also bake our own bread.

Pro Tip

Cooking is chemistry. As in a science lab, everything has to work in concert to reach an absolute outcome. When I am preparing desserts, I like to get all the eggs, cream cheese, butter, and the like to room temperature to give them better texture, volume, and consistency. Butter pulled cold out of the fridge is much harder to cook with, and you tend to end up with fragments in the dough. By definition, "room temperature" is typically about 70 degrees, so be mindful of your kitchen temperature. Use this tip at home, too.

Q You noted you will actually leave the kitchen on occasion and rush to the nearest grocery store if Nick & Sam's does not have something a guest really wants. How can you keep up that sort of thing?

SAMIR: Ha! Yes, we'll do anything to keep guests happy. But after this happens, we will have a chef or a manager go by the table and give the customer a card and say, "The next time, give us a call, and we'll be happy to make it for you."

Q Did you ever have a moment when you wondered if you were in the wrong business?

SAMIR: Oh, we all have bad days. But no, not really. When I was in New York, I did wonder if I was in the right town since I was broke all the time. For a long time, I worked from 8 a.m. to 4 p.m. at Sfuzzi, which was at 65th and Ninth and then would trudge across that 65th Street Bridge over Central Park for a mile-and-a-third walk to Sign of the Dove restaurant at 66th and Third, where I'd work from 4:30 p.m. to 12:30 a.m. That got old. No matter how many hours I put in, it seemed like I always had to dig in my pocket for change to buy ciga-rettes. I was burning out. After Sfuzzi, I took a break and was just a line cook at a few places, including Tribeca Grill, which by the way was co-owned by the great Robert De Niro, who made many personal appearances back in the kitchen. But I was still excited to be learning about food, and I never regretted getting into this business.

Q People ask you if you've ever considered opening your own place. What do you tell them?

SAMIR: I ask, "Why should I?" I already have the greatest gig and the best staff imaginable. They really make me a superstar. I am also a part owner, and I can walk in and walk out anytime I please. No schedule. I am truly blessed here.

Q The world is ending. What would your last meal be?

SAMIR: That's easy. My mother's lentils and rice. It's a simple dish that only she could make elegant. It's drizzled with a clarified Indian butter called ghee and served with papadum, a fried flatbread. Add a homemade mango pickle, and you're ready to go. But if I was really rushed and had to go the fast-food route, you'd find me at a Gray's Papaya in New York with a big hot dog in my hand.

Pro Tip

It's all about the "kids." I'm not talking about the elementary-school or junior-high set, though you certainly want to give this impressionable group a special experience as well as the parents who are picking up the tabs. The kids I refer to here are young adults. If you don't appeal to today's fickle young consumers, you are, for want of a better word, cooked. The minute this generation doesn't get exactly what they want in food, atmosphere, personalized service, or whatever else (including tolerance of casual dress), they'll go elsewhere. When we ask our managers to chat up guests to determine what they like and want and vice-versa, we always talk with our established regulars of course, but we never skip the kids. They're our next-generation diner. I'm sure you've been to somber, old-school restaurants patronized solely by older diners. What's wrong with this picture? Well, when this demographic is gone, so is the restaurant! You have to constantly adapt to emerging generations.

Q **Where is your happy place to get away from it all?**
SAMIR: On a personal level, it's with my family. Aside from that, I'm already where I love to be when I step in the door at Nick & Sam's. I truly am. When I overhear someone at work telling another worker to chill out and go to their "happy place," I can't help but think that I'm already in my happy place. I have the best job in the world.

Lori, Mia, Cole, and Samir on a family vacation

CHAPTER 7

The Founder's Tale
(and other takes)

Phil Romano, creator of Nick & Sam's and twenty-nine other concepts:

Nick & Sam's would not have evolved into the culinary force it is today without our star chef, Samir Dhurandhar. I've always said that imagination and wonder have no limits, and Samir illustrates this on a daily basis as well as any hire I've ever made.

Samir has been with me since the restaurant's inception. I've watched him repeatedly go well beyond the call of duty as our executive chef and partner, busting his butt daily until the wee hours to make sure every detail is tended to, every meal is completed to perfection, and all our valued customers leave satisfied—and full.

But before I hired him as executive chef, I was more than a little skeptical about one thing in particular: Here was a chef from India, seeking to take command of an American steakhouse kitchen. There would be no sacred cows at

101

Nick & Sam's—except for our patrons. So, when I met Samir, I wasted no time in getting to the point: "Are you going to have a problem cooking meat?" I asked. He responded, "No, Mr. Romano, I am new-generation Indian. I cook meat and crave meat, and I just love the way it smells when it's sizzling on the grill. My father and my siblings ate meat, and I have been cooking it since I was a child. It has always been an art form for me, and a big part of what I am as a chef."

What a relief! That's exactly what I needed to hear because I had a good feeling about this guy from the moment I met him. So, I told him, "Okay, Samir, I'll give you this shot to prove yourself, and if it works out, then you can build a future here. It will all depend on how happy you make people." And man, talk about happy. In fact, Samir takes care of people so well, they always remember him and come back again and again, and they tell others about their experience. He's the one who really gets everybody hooked on his food.

I also love the fact that Samir is the ultimate family guy and has the support of his beautiful wife and kids. I admire that stability in him and the way his former employers and colleagues speak about him. If I'm considering hiring or promoting someone who has been divorced or fired multiple times, it always makes me wonder how he can be successful with me if he can't be successful in life.

But let me back up a bit. To give you a true picture of why Samir fits in so well in this one-of-a-kind place, I will need to give you more of the Nick & Sam's backstory.

As Samir has told you, my restaurant career goes back a ways. I opened the first of my thirty restaurant concepts, The Gladiator, in 1965 in Lake Park, Florida, at age 24, on money from my father, Sam. He literally bet the family home on me, taking out a second mortgage, so failure was not an option.

I eventually launched several national concepts that you may have dined at, such as Romano's Macaroni Grill, Fuddruckers, Rudy's Country Store and Bar-B-Q, and eatZi's—all well before I founded Nick & Sam's.

I cooked up the idea for Nick & Sam's because the downtown Dallas/Lower Uptown area really needed a first-class steakhouse with a lively culture—not another one of those darkened old-school joints where everyone speaks in hushed tones. In fact, I have a saying that's carried over to all my restaurant creations: If you want a nice quiet dinner, go to a funeral home.

I've always felt that diners want to be a part of a happy and upbeat crowd—a gallery of sorts—in a great restaurant. They like the social excitement, the positive energy, and the feeling of being privy to a good thing.

So, with this in mind and an excellent location—a former Lawry's The Prime Rib space a little north of the central business district—I began visualizing how my new brainchild was going to operate, and I slowly started piecing my team together.

But I was about sixty years old and approaching the twilight of my career, and I wasn't really anxious to put in those twelve- to fourteen-hour days that it really takes to get an exceptional restaurant off the ground. So, I'd need to bring in a "sweat equity" partner to help share the burden. As it happened, Sfuzzi cofounder Patrick Columbo lived in Dallas, and he told me he wanted to operate a restaurant company there. That was exactly what I needed, so I had my partner.

We also needed a distinguished name for this steakhouse, in part because I visualized it sticking around for a very long time—long after I am gone. As it happened, Patrick and his wife had just had a baby boy named Nick. And my son, Samuel (named after his granddad), was just a toddler at the time, so we combined them. But "Sam & Nick's" sounded a little rough around the edges. In fact, the name evoked thoughts of an extermination team—and, we joked, not the insect-killing variety. So, we transposed the names. "Nick & Sam's" just rolled off the tongue—no small consideration for a place that gets some of the best—if not *the* best—word-of-mouth buzz I've seen in my career.

But I also needed some other new blood, ideally with edgy, creative talent and a flair for the unconventional, to run my kitchen and floor. I had never worked with either Samir or the GM before I brought them aboard. But, I thought, maybe that was good. I wanted fresh viewpoints on this thing, and these guys came on board with strong recommendations out of restaurants in ultra-competitive metro areas. And they fit the "new blood" bill.

And, of course, Samir came with his own impressive skills and culinary pedigree. It's important to note that I brought in Samir well before there was a place for him to ply his considerable craft because the finish out on the physical restaurant would take the better part of a year. In the meantime, I had Samir, Patrick, and a couple of our other folks over to my Dallas house for daily meetings so we could collectively brainstorm and build the concept in our minds. We'd all sit down, and I'd just say, "Okay, start talking" in my customary terse way. And there they went: There was no shortage of ideas.

Samir would cook up a wide assortment of steak, fish, fowl, and lamb treatments and side dishes in my home kitchen, using his own innate creativity and our input. We "tested" these with eagerness, but as good as they were, we all came to an opinion that these weren't quite right for what we were planning. We continued to experiment as we mulled over what seemed like a million other little details.

We wondered if we should offer combination dinners—ones that included predetermined sides. No. Ultimately, we didn't want to tie our hands or those of the customer by pushing anything they didn't want nor did we want to screw around with constant substitutions. That's not the clientele we were after anyway. Should we offer lunch? Again, no. Let's focus on one thing—dinner—but do that one thing better than anybody.

We arrived at a dinner-only à la carte menu with a lengthy list of sides, unlike the typical handful of standard steakhouse accompaniments. And for the steaks? They had to be the pinnacle of the industry. We tried a variety of premium meats from different vendors, but Allen Brothers, founded in 1893, stood out. Their hand selection, hand cutting, aging process, and custom portioning of meats stood out. There's a reason they've been around for a century and a quarter. Of course, Allen Brothers is more expensive, as you would expect, but we weren't about to cut corners at our new Uptown steakhouse. Expectations are always huge for a Romano concept, so there could be nothing average here (and that would include the average check price!).

The place would also need a distinctive ambiance. To raise a few eyebrows, I decided to put a baby grand piano right on the edge of the kitchen to serve as a conversation piece. We installed an enormous, spectacular chandelier in

Sam Romano and Phil Romano at Sam's college graduation surprise party

the heart of the main dining area, raised multiple wine walls to section off the dining floor, and splashed the other walls with art deco murals and vivid paintings. (Disclosure: Okay, some of the pieces are my own, from my Samuel Lynne Galleries in Dallas, although guests don't know it unless they ask.)

Nick & Sam's cost us about $3.4 million to get up and running. That's a pretty substantial restaurant investment even for these days, much less for back in 1999.

We opened that spring with no advertising, letting our talent-laden staff do their magic. We brought in culinary heavyweights like the flashy Nick Badovinus as Samir's executive sous chef and Dennis Renna, a former Brinker International corporate chef, as founding maître d'.

Our steakhouse was an instant hit, and the place seemed to advance on its own momentum. "If it stays this good through dessert," writer Mark Stuertz observed in the *Dallas Observer* just after we opened, "this place will tear Dallas' steakhouses a new vent between the rump roasts."

After about a year, Patrick and I had some operating disagreements, dissolved our partnership, and went our separate ways, but we remain on good terms. The place still bears his son's name, along with my son's. And Sam has been very active in the restaurant following his graduation from Syracuse and studied all facets of the business for years before he finally took over my ownership stake in 2022.

The restaurant has suffered a few blips along the way, but as Samir noted, things really took off after Super Bowl XLV was in town in February 2011 and never let up from there. Once people found us, they returned again and again and again—even if they were in town for only a single night each time.

From the beginning, our intent was to sell more than just great food at Nick & Sam's. And we continue to do just that. With every seating, we sell high energy, atmosphere, art, showmanship, and sexiness. It's where the beautiful people can be seen and see one another. Our bar scene is one of the best in the city, and a lot of celebs love to hang around there.

The many movers and shakers who are so in love with Samir's cooking (and our rare wines) have fallen head over heels for the cachet and culture, too, as have the many patrons from all walks of life who like to drink in the rarified atmosphere as they splurge on a magnificent meal and experience. People looking for the time of their lives for birthdays or special occasions seem to choose us.

It turns out that my instinct to offer ownership shares of Nick & Sam's to Samir was right on. Throughout my restaurant career, I've discovered that giving ownership to the right people provides added incentive and always translates to superior customer service. "Why do it just for me when you can do it for yourself," I ask them. That's the ultimate motivator. Work for yourself.

At first, I lingered around Nick & Sam's to make sure the guys didn't make any mistakes. But now, I am basically there for the food. Samir and other managers know a hell of a lot more about running the place than I do now, and, frankly, I am glad. Before I pulled back, my overriding instruction to them was simple: Keep the culture. Today, Samir and crew do just that, and he gets the final say in any changes and other big decisions, as well he should.

Nick & Sam's will always have a special place in my heart; the connection to my son will be everlasting. One day, when Sam was about four, I asked him what he'd say when he is older and owned the place. "Welcome to my restaurant," he exclaimed. "I hope you enjoy the food."

A few years later, I took him back into the kitchen and told him we were going to wash dishes to practice up for his later roles at Nick & Sam's. He said, "But, Dad, I'm not going to work back here. I want to work with the maître d'." I said, "But, Sam, I want you to. What's wrong?" In a frustrated tone, he said, "Dad, I can't speak Mexican!" I laughed. So, he ended up working with the maître d', a guy named Tony, and somehow—I guess cuteness goes a long way— he wangled a $13 tip. Tony told him, "Hey, Sam, you gotta split that with me." Sam retorted, "Well, if you treated people nice like me, you'd get your own tip."

We've always been a fun place and even slightly irreverent, but Nick & Sam's set a little more sophisticated tone at first, instilling a dress code: jackets required, etc. But, over the years, we relaxed that, as modern diners, driven by the preferences of the younger casual crowd, wanted to wear their jeans and other casual attire to further relax while dining out.

While guests may not dress to the nines anymore, some of our biggest customers still spend astonishing sums. We sometimes just shake our heads and wonder where the hell they got that sort of dough.

Case in point: A few years ago, one guy brought in a big entourage for a posh party to celebrate the sale of his Dallas company. And the sky—or should I say the stratosphere—was the limit. He ordered loads of everything, including our most expensive vintages, side after side after side, steak after steak, lobster after lobster, dessert after dessert. He had apparently made millions from his big divestiture; and man, he came ready to party.

His bill? Are you sitting down? It was $80,000! And no, that's not a typo. But that's not the end of the story. The 80 grand didn't include his tip, which was a generous and jaw-dropping 37.5%, or $30,000. The waiter was basically a brand-new guy, and he was just floored when he saw the tally. The next week, he quit and went back to school!

People will spend money on quality. It was Samir's idea to later do the exclusive Wagyu menu, and we've become known far and wide for it. It gave us an added dimension that few others had and another point of difference for a clientele that wants the best. People don't mind paying a high price point for something that is truly unique and authentic.

So, I am content to leave one of my proudest achievements in the hands of Samir and team—and my son. I expect their grandkids to dine there some day.

Chef Sam Hazen

Sam Hazen, culinary director/executive chef at The Highlawn, consultant to the Culinary Institute of America, and former executive chef for Tao restaurants, Veritas, and others:

I first met the talented and passionate Samir Dhurandhar at the Culinary Institute of America in upstate New York in 1990, when I was a newly appointed instructor and still a very young chef.

It was a little daunting for Samir at first, coming from India with minimal knowledge of domestic cuisine, foodstuffs, and the complex US restaurant culture. In my years at the institute, in fact, I can't recall another native-Indian student. So, Samir's challenges were many.

But his passion for learning and his ability to open his mind to absorb new techniques, flavors, and styles quickly overcame any deficit—and then some.

Plus, he had the built-in advantage of hailing from a land where flavors are life.

At the CIA, as the institute is known, I would get a new class of sixteen to eighteen students every seven to fourteen days, so it was tough for a new student to stand out. With each class, I would analyze what skills the students had and what it would take for them to succeed in a very tough industry. I'd also look at their initiative to learn and openness to new cooking techniques.

Unfortunately, too many of the kids would come in thinking they already knew everything. But not Samir. As I got to know him at the CIA, I'd often tell myself, "This guy has the drive, the ability to grow, and the passion. He can go far."

Samir was a rarity in that way—like a knowledge sponge. What's more, he was humble with a gentle demeanor, determined to learn from his mistakes, plus he wanted to know everything about the profession. He studiously watched every move I made. I am a driven person, and I recognized that in Samir on day one.

Seeing his great potential, I stuck on him like glue. As a young chef, Samir's climb to greatness was inevitable, and I wanted to be a part of it. I felt a responsibility to help him shine as a chef and to tell him all I knew—good or bad. Why?

Because, as in sports, when any coach worth his salt recognizes a great player with amazing potential, he goes out of his way to afford him extra attention. Hence, every step of Samir's career became extremely important to me, and not surprisingly, he enjoyed immediate success upon graduation. (And I know he nurtures budding chefs today as I did for him.)

It's no surprise that Samir will stop at nothing to please the customer. He will literally run out to his car and race to the grocery store if one of his customers wants something that the restaurant doesn't have. Who does that? Only a person like Samir, and there aren't many of them.

Samir is the guy that people just want to have on their team. His presence resonates throughout the restaurant. Talk with Nick & Sam's busboys, bartenders, sous chefs, the people in the dish room, the wait station, or the grill station—anybody—and you feel it. He's widely respected and emulated, and that doesn't happen by mistake. You don't get respect. You earn respect.

Samir is also a guy who exudes sincerity and that goes a long way in trust building. There are very few people I trust, but Samir is definitely one of them. He walks the talk with no phoniness or BS. If there was a dipstick that we could use on people to see how real they are, Samir's would be at the "full" mark.

When you talk with Samir, it's impossible to not smile. And his passion for his profession? Look up the definition of the word, and it will say, "See Samir."

After his student days, we became chef friends and real-life friends, and we remain so today, keeping in touch wherever fate lands us. As a New Yorker, I'm a hardened New York Giants fan who travels once a year to Dallas for their game with the Cowboys. I always let Samir know I'm coming so we'll be sure to catch up. Then, he'll say such things as, "Sam, is there anything you need? Can I get you a hotel room?"

That's just the way he is, like a close family member. If he called me when I was in town and said, "Hey, a busboy didn't show tonight, can you come in?" I wouldn't hesitate for a second.

There are a lot of amazing chefs in Dallas, but Samir just stands out. Seeing his evolution is gratifying. Not only that, but Samir has also grown to be a wonderful family man as well as a fantastic asset to Nick & Sam's and his community. I am absolutely thrilled he's in the position he's in.

Samir's Texas license plate

Samir is the whole package: a star pupil, star chef, and star friend.

Jim Migliorini (brewmaster), Samir, Unknown Chef, Richard Pietromonico

Richard Pietromonico, executive chef, Houston Hall, and former corporate chef, Sfuzzi and Heartland Brewery:

S amir Dhurandhar and I met at a job fair in 1993 when he studied at the
Culinary Institute of America in Hyde Park, New York, known affection-
ately as the CIA. I was the corporate chef at Sfuzzi in Manhattan at the time and
was always scouting for new talent.

Of course, the institute had a wealth of promising young, hungry students
looking for that big break. I know that well because I was once one of them; I
had graduated from the CIA seven years before. Students spend an intensive two
years of training there, and, though they come out a bit unseasoned as all new
grads do, they typically have a strong foundation in food preparation and know
their way around a commercial-size kitchen.

I took a liking to Samir instantly; it was clear he had a real passion for the culinary arts that went all the way back to his youth. Not only that, but he was also humble and well-spoken, had a lot of energy, and just seemed like a very nice guy—the kind that would fit well in the Sfuzzi culture, I thought. I left the institute that day with a good impression of Samir in my mind and basically knew I was going to hire him before I sent formal word a few days later. (Ironically, we went on to hire a second Samir from the institute.)

Though the first Samir had just graduated from a prestigious culinary school, he never acted like he knew more than he did. Instead, he was like a sponge, absorbing everything I taught him, wide-eyed, constantly asking me good questions. He was just a joy to train.

Samir always learned from his mistakes, as do the best. But he didn't make too many of them. I know he'll hate that I'm saying this, but I do recall that once, after he had just arrived, he tried to cool a batch of fresh Italian rigatoni that we were going to use for hot pasta by rinsing it off with cold water, which is a no-no. It should never be rinsed, just drained, because the starchy film helps the sauce cling to, and get absorbed by, the pasta, I told him. Pasta salad, on the other hand, can be rinsed. He quickly recognized his faux pas, and I'm sure he never repeated it. I only bring it up because he was so damn good at everything else.

In fact, Samir's creative touch in the kitchen became so obvious that he was eventually given latitude to come up with his own menu items, something chefs just weren't allowed to do at other Sfuzzi locations. And he did quite well with them. After we each left Sfuzzi, he worked with me in a few of my other ventures. He just lays it on the line every night.

I am very proud of Samir and applaud his rousing success. Though it sounds trite, it truly couldn't happen to a nicer guy. He is just a stand-up person and a true-blue family man. The fact that he attributes some of his well-deserved good fortune to me is very flattering. He has earned everything he has with hard work.

CHAPTER 8

A Toast to My
Two Families

I t's Samir again. As I complete these reflections, the restaurant industry continues to reel from the pain of COVID-19 as the virus and its variants enter a fourth year of living among us. Countless restaurants—as many as 100,000-plus—have closed in the US since 2020, and more are teetering on the brink. We need you to get out and support them for the sake of the industry's future. So, eat, drink, and be merry—dine-in or carry-out—for tomorrow we must dine.

I want to offer a toast here, not only to the Nick & Sam's family who helped complete me as a chef but also to the loved ones who truly complete me as a human being: my own lovely family. That would be wife Lori, daughter Mia, and son Cole. They continue to inspire, delight, and support me in so many ways.

There are still days when I put in ten to fifteen hours at work and am scarce at home, so I am very appreciative of their patience and understanding. Of course, I don't *have* to put in these hours, but there's no getting around the fact that this is a hands-on, labor-intensive business if you want to get it right.

While I sound like a workaholic, I take off Sundays and Mondays each week with rare exceptions. Apart from a couple of swims in our pool and a massage, my "weekend" is all family time, which includes copious home cooking, which is something I enjoy greatly in our tranquil home setting away from the Nick & Sam's frenzy. No matter how rough a day (or week) I've faced, there's always the oasis of my home and family, including our cat and three dogs, to return to.

Samir, Lori, Mia, and Cole

A little background on the fam: I met my wife, Lori, at the restaurant in 1999, not long after Nick & Sam's opened. But our connection really began, appropriately, over a meal on the eve of the big Y2K New Year's changeover.

The best friend of one my Nick & Sam's regulars, it turns out, had a roommate who happened to be my friend, too. The two, I'm sure, shared intel about how I remained miserably unattached.

So, they cooked up a New Year's Eve plan that would bring a mutual female friend of theirs over to my place in the afternoon, ostensibly as a tagalong, to wish me an early Happy New Year. But they called an "audible." Their idea: How about they and this beautiful young lady named Lori, whom I had met only briefly at the restaurant, *fixing dinner for me* that New Year's Eve to give me a break from cooking? Well, okay. I went along with the idea. And man, am I glad I did. Lori, as you've no doubt guessed, would eventually become my bride!

But I confess, there was a little early friction that night. You see, as enticing as it was to have others cook for me, I'm more than a little particular about any and all food preparation as you know, and I'm just flat-out tough to keep out of the kitchen, especially my own kitchen.

So, I may have been hovering *just a little*. And I couldn't help but notice Lori was struggling to peel a stubborn, rigid clove of garlic. If you read my earlier tip on this very subject, then you'll understand why I proceeded to gently suggest to Lori that she could simply immerse that pesky clove in warm water for a while, and it would then easily separate from its skin. So, I, ahem, did. And I don't exaggerate when I say this: Lori shot me one of the nastiest looks I've ever received.

Fearing a far less flattering suggestion in return, I quickly retreated, content to let Lori continue her noble battle with the clove. I certainly didn't want to grow into disfavor with this lovely young lady, especially since she had been kind enough to cook for me. (Alright, another confession: I noticed she was really hot!)

Later, as we indulged in New Year's Eve libations, Lori, who was gracious enough to forgive my early meddling, and I got to talking and seemed to connect on so many different levels.

At this point, my eyes were wide open, and I was feeling a spark. But was she?

We talked several more times by phone following that night and met up again, and things went smoothly. The Super Bowl was right around the corner, so I seized the opportunity to proffer Lori an invite to watch the big game at a friend's party. She agreed. My good fortune!

We arrived early and started drinking, paying only passive attention to the game when it finally came on. Afterwards, the two of us went for a nosh and a nightcap at Primo's—now called Primo's MX Kitchen & Lounge—one of my favorite little Dallas Tex-Mex spots on McKinney Avenue.

Time passed like a flash. A small-town girl who had moved to Dallas after graduating from college, Lori had a great down-to-earth quality. We took down a few bottles of wine at Primo's, then a couple more, then another. It was a blur. But somehow, I wasn't intoxicated—except by her! We couldn't keep our eyes off each other.

We closed the place down and headed toward her place. I would have been content to just walk her to the door, but steps away from it, she suddenly turned and kissed me passionately. Mutual sparks! I was smitten, to say the least.

Since that night, Lori has been my closest confidante, my rock and spiritual inspiration. She's beautiful, kind, and fun, and she graciously acknowledges— well, usually!—that my Nick & Sam's world is my bread and butter and knows the kind of sweat equity and dedication I need to put out to make it all work. Most people outside of the business don't—or won't—grasp that. Always a giving person, Lori worked as a sonographer and mammographer until our beautiful kids came along.

Our daughter, Mia, who will be nineteen in July 2023, is the oldest. She adores animals and has worked at a boarding kennel. She has wanted to be a

Lori and Samir at their engagement party

teacher since she was little. Our son, Cole, who will be seventeen in September 2023, is an excellent athlete and plays center in football with dreams to play through college. He works at a diner on weekends.

But I'd be remiss to not mention the myriad connections and opportunities I've had with my other family—the Nick & Sam's one—to build menus for other concepts. Over the years, I've been honored to create menus or partial menus for some of Phil's successes, such as The Network Bar (Deviled Eggs with Crispy Shrimp and Andouille Sausage, anyone?), the Kobe beef–influenced Who's Who Burger in Highland Park, the distinct Dos Jefes Latin-Asian fusion tapas concept, and a few others.

In September of 2021, I launched my own exciting off-premises venture, a full-service catering company called Savor by Samir. It was something I'd been wanting to do for years, not only to expand creatively but also to offer customers additional and reliable food offerings for their fundraisers, family weddings, company events, special Sunday suppers, private parties, and the like.

It all became possible because Phil and his son, Sam, happened to own the lease on a catering kitchen (not far from Phil's Samuel Lynne Galleries on Dragon Street) that wasn't being used much. So, Savor was born! Our motto is "creative ideas, professional staff, and sensational food," and we serve all that up with years of experience, elegance, and expertise—and I'm proud to say, in a seamless and harmonious manner. People expect no less of me.

As I've put these recollections together, it's been a joy to consider the many wonderful people who've advised me, aided me, and inspired me. I guess it really goes back to Julia Child and my chance meeting with her three decades ago in Uncle Bob's kitchen, with me still dripping wet from the swimming pool.

It was then that she encouraged this impressionable Indian lad to attend the Culinary Institute of America. I told you how I ran into Julia again at culinary school a year or so after our first meeting, as she signed her enormously influential cooking books, and how she greeted me warmly by name, with no prompting. As the years went by, I thought of her often, resigned that I would never see her again.

But, my God, there she was in Dallas for a large national culinary convention in 2002, attending a luncheon in our private-party room at Nick & Sam's. When I heard she was on the premises, I rushed to greet her. As I entered the room, there she was—nearly ninety at the time though still easily recognizable— the grand queen of French cuisine, sitting tall at the head of table.

I said a robust hello and reintroduced myself. But try as I may, I just couldn't jog her memory about our history. She apologized, complaining that such lapses were becoming common with her age and medications. But as in our previous conversations, Julia said something that filled my heart with delight: "But, Samir, these are the best French fries I have ever had in my life."

Ha! Yes! As the ultimate US master of French cuisine, she would know.

We had a delightful visit and finally bid each other adieu. She passed away in 2004, but her legacy will endure worldwide, with so many movies and shows touching on the food-culture revolution she authored. I was thrilled to see the show based on her life, *Julia*, which now airs on HBO Max.

I had gone full circle with my idol and early adviser. What a blessing she was to me and to every chef who sought to make themselves known. She brought the potential for stardom and honor to all of us in this very challenging profession.

So, in honor of Julia's "best French fry" proclamation, just ask your server for a gratis order of Damn Good Fries next time you're in Nick & Sam's anytime through 2024. And you can thank Julia!

There's more excitement to come. We are pondering plans to grow the Nick & Sam's concept to a select few locations around the country, though COVID has kept those on the back burner. Still, opening a New York location would bring me full circle in another way. After all, New York was where I earned my culinary degree, got my professional start, and had the honor of cooking the big James Beard dinner. So, stay tuned.

This autobiography was fun for me and hopefully edifying and appetizing for you. Remember, nothing in this business—or any business—replaces hard work, attention to detail, ethics, and an all-out dedication to the customers and staff. And nothing beats a great meal prepared by Nick & Sam's. We'll keep the kitchen piano tuned for you!

Recipes by Samir

I am often asked for my recipes, which is easier said than done. I mostly cook by instinct and memory. But here, I have gathered for you recipes from my James Beard House menu, the Swanky Chophouse (still one of the most incredible experiences of my professional life), family recipes from my mom, and of course, a few Nick and Sam's favorites.

If you are adventurous in the kitchen, I hope you will give these recipes a try. If you are an armchair cook, enjoy!

Award-Winning James Beard House Dinner Recipes— Swanky Chophouse

All Beard dinner recipes serve 8 to 12

Crispy Oyster Gougères with Barbecued Beef Bacon

Crispy Oysters

60	shucked raw oysters	3	cups vegetable oil
1	cup milk, at room temperature		Salt to taste
2	cups flour seasoned with salt and pepper		

1. Heat oil in saucepan until temperature reads 375 degrees.
2. In a mixing bowl, toss the oysters in the milk.
3. Dip the oysters in the flour mixture.
4. Deep-fry until crisp. Season with salt.

Barbecued Beef Bacon

5	pounds sliced beef bacon	2	cups barbecue sauce

1. Preheat oven to 375 degrees
2. Arrange the bacon on a sheet pan with a rack. Bake until it starts getting crisp.
3. Brush the barbecue sauce on the bacon. Put the bacon back in the oven and bake until crisp.
4. Remove the bacon from the oven. Let stand to cool. Cut into bite-size pieces.

Gougères

3	cups water	12	eggs
1	cup plus 2 tablespoons butter	1½	cups shredded Gruyère cheese
9	teaspoons sugar	2	ounces fresh thyme
3	teaspoons salt	1	teaspoon pepper
2¼	cups flour		

1. Heat water, butter, sugar, and salt. Bring to a boil.
2. Add flour and mix vigorously until flour starts separating itself from the edges. Cook over medium heat for about 8 minutes.
3. Stir in eggs one at a time until all are dissolved.
4. Add cheese, thyme, and pepper.
5. Remove and put into piping (pastry) bag with a star tip.
6. Pipe small rosettes (about 1 inch wide and 1½ inches tall) onto a sheet pan with parchment.
7. Bake at 400 degrees for 15 minutes.

Apple Fennel Slaw

2	Pink Lady or Gala apples	1	head fennel
1	cup celery leaves		Tarragon Vinaigrette (below)

1. Julienne the apples, pick the celery leaves, and shave the fennel. Place in a mixing bowl and toss together.
2. Toss in Tarragon Vinaigrette.

Tarragon Vinaigrette

2	ounces fresh tarragon	1	teaspoon sugar
2	ounces apple cider vinegar	1	teaspoon lemon juice
3	ounces extra-virgin olive oil		Sea salt to taste

1. Blend all ingredients in a blender.
2. Reserve in the refrigerator.

RECIPE CONTINUES ON NEXT PAGE

Smokra Aïoli

Smokra, including juice   **Shallots**

Mayonnaise   **Sea salt**

1. Chop smokra.
2. Add mayonnaise, shallots, smokra juice, and sea salt and stir gently.

Final Assembly

1. Toss Apple Fennel Slaw and lay out 6 small mounds on a plate.
2. Cut the gougères in half, reserving the lids.
3. Put the crisp oysters into the gougères, top with Smokra Aioli, and top with a piece of Barbecued Beef Bacon. Top the gougères with the lids at an angle to expose the bacon and oyster.
4. Place the 6 gougères on the slaw.
5. Serve hot.

Crab Cake Poppers

2 cups mascarpone

1 pound jumbo or colossal crabmeat

6 ounces shallots, chopped

1 bunch cilantro, chopped

2 ounces green chilies, chopped

2 cups tempura flour (and water to make batter)

Tomato Preserves (below)

1. Mix mascarpone, crabmeat, shallots, cilantro, and green chilies.
2. Season to taste.
3. Shape mixture into small balls (about ¾ ounce each).
4. Chill prepared balls in refrigerator for 2 hours.
5. Make tempura batter by mixing tempura flour with just enough cold water to create a smooth, thick batter.
6. Heat oil in saucepot to about 350 degrees.
7. Remove balls from chiller. Using a fork, dip balls into tempura batter.
8. Deep-fry in oil until golden and crispy. Serve with the Tomato Preserves.

Tomato Preserves

10 Roma tomatoes

2 lemons, thinly sliced

2 cups sugar

1. Score tomatoes at the base with a crisscross.
2. Heat a saucepot with water and bring to a boil.
3. Add the tomatoes and cook for 6 to 8 minutes or until the skin starts peeling back.
4. Strain tomatoes and add to ice water to stop the cooking process.
5. Peel, seed, and chop the tomatoes
6. Add tomatoes to a saucepot, including the juices.
7. Add lemon slices and sugar. Cook on medium to low flame for 30 minutes.

Chicken Liver Crostini

1   baguette

2   ounces extra-virgin olive oil

1   ounce chopped garlic

Chicken Liver Mousse (below)

Port Jelly (at right)

1. Cut baguettes diagonally on a bias.
2. Brush with extra-virgin olive oil.
3. Rub with garlic.
4. Toast in oven at 350 degrees for 8 minutes.
5. Serve the crostini with the Chicken Liver Mousse and Port Jelly on the side.

Chicken Liver Mousse

½   pound butter, softened, plus 2 ounces melted butter

2   ounces finely chopped shallots

3   ounces finely chopped white anchovies

2   ounces finely chopped capers

1   ounce finely chopped garlic

6   ounces chicken livers (cleaned)

4   ounces white wine

1   ounce finely chopped thyme

1. Melt butter in a sauté pan on low to medium heat.
2. Add shallots, anchovies, capers, and garlic.
3. Sauté until aroma develops.
4. Add chicken livers and turn heat up high.
5. Caramelize chicken livers.
6. Add white wine and thyme.
7. Reduce wine until nearly evaporated.
8. Season mousse to taste.
9. Remove from heat and cool slightly.
10. Purée in food processer until smooth.
11. Pass through a fine China cap strainer.

12. Put into a ramekin and pour melted butter over the mousse.
13. Refrigerate.

Port Jelly

3   cups port

1¼ cups sugar

2   pounds fresh figs, cut in half

3   leaves gelatin (softened in ice cold water)

1. Place all ingredients in a saucepot.
2. Bring to a boil.
3. Reduce heat to simmer and reduce sauce by a third.
4. Season and reserve.

Eggplant Papadum

18 mini papadum

1 eggplant

2 ounces butter

1 yellow onion, peeled and finely chopped

½ ounce garlic, chopped

½ ounce ginger, chopped

½ ounce garam masala

½ ounce dried fenugreek leaves

1 ounce shredded coconut

½ bunch cilantro, chopped

1. Fry papadum until crisp and golden. Reserve.
2. Char eggplant on open flame on stovetop.
3. Cool slightly. Peel and reserve the flesh.
4. Melt butter in saucepan. Sauté onion, garlic, and ginger.
5. Add eggplant purée.
6. Season with garam masala, fenugreek, and coconut.
7. Add cilantro and cook until dry.
8. Season and reserve.

Allen Brothers Prime Filet and Bluefin Toro with Caviar, Truffles, and Pickled Fresno Chiles

4   ounces bluefin toro, sliced into ½-ounce pieces

8   ounces prime filet, sliced into 1-ounce slices

1   ounce black sturgeon Osetra caviar

8   black truffle slices

4   ounces ponzu sauce

Pickled Fresno Chilies (below)

Micro cilantro as needed

1. Wrap the toro with the slices of beef.
2. Top with caviar and truffle slices.
3. Add ponzu to the plate.
4. Top with Pickled Fresno Chilies and micro cilantro.

Time: 10 minutes

Pickled Fresno Chilies

1   cup sherry vinegar

1   cup sugar

2   bay leaves

1   ounce whole coriander

1   ounce cumin seed

10 garlic cloves

10 black peppercorns

3   cups sliced Fresno chilies

1. Combine ingredients in a saucepot.
2. Bring to a boil and pour over Fresno chilies.
3. Reserve.

Australian Wagyu Short Rib Cannelloni with Reggiano Fonduta and San Marzano Tomatoes

Short Ribs

6   pounds short ribs

Olive oil

1   stalk leek, chopped

3   ounces shallots, chopped

8   ounces cremini mushrooms, sliced

4   ounces carrot, chopped

4   ounces celery, chopped

3   ounces garlic, chopped

4   cups red wine

1   cup red wine vinegar

2   (14-ounce) cans whole San Marzano tomatoes, crushed

10   cups veal stock or chicken stock

2   stalks rosemary

½   bunch thyme

4   ounces grated truffle pecorino cheese

4   ounces mascarpone

2   ounces assorted fresh herbs, chopped

1. Sear ribs in olive oil.
2. Sauté leek, shallots, mushrooms, carrot, celery, and garlic.
3. Add red wine, red wine vinegar, and San Marzano tomatoes. Reduce completely.
4. Add veal or chicken stock, rosemary, and thyme.
5. Braise until totally tender. Remove from the liquid. Cool and shred.
6. Separately, reduce the liquid (sauce).
7. To make the mixture, add some sauce, grated truffle pecorino, whipped mascarpone, and herbs to ribs.

Crespelle

1   cup flour

2   eggs

| ½ | teaspoon salt | | Nutmeg |
| 1 | cup milk | | |

1. Mix ingredients.
2. Make crepes.

Reggiano Fonduta

8	ounces fontina, grated	4	egg yolks
2	ounces Reggiano, grated		Sliced truffle
1	cup milk		Nutmeg
4	tablespoons butter		

1. Soak cheeses in milk overnight.
2. Melt butter in skillet. Add cheese mix.
3. Once melted, add egg yolks, sliced truffle, and nutmeg.
4. Cook over a double boiler.

Tomato Shallot Compote

| Shallots | Thyme |
| Garlic oil | Roma tomatoes |

1. Halve shallots and roast with garlic oil and thyme slowly until soft.
2. Roast Roma tomatoes with thyme and balsamic vinegar slowly until soft. Mix and season.

Final Assembly (in order)

1. Tomato Shallot Compote
2. Stuffed Crespelle with Short Ribs (warmed)
3. Fonduta
4. Truffle

Total time: 4 hours

Little Gem Caesar Salad with Crisp Eggs and Bottarga

The Lettuce

1. Grill half a head of lettuce. Leave the other half raw.

Dijon Vinaigrette

1. Combine Dijon, anchovy, lemon juice, white wine vinegar, garlic, olive oil, sea salt.

Brown Butter Croutons

1. Brown butter by cooking it past melting point, toss with brioche cubes, bake until crisp, and season with Parmesan and salt.

Crisp Eggs

1. Poach quail eggs. Bread the eggs with flour, egg, and breadcrumbs. Deep-fry.

Final Assembly

1. Mix the grilled and raw lettuce.
2. Shave bottarga. Add vinaigrette, eggs, croutons, and bottarga.

Time: 30 minutes

Chilean Sea Bass with Tikka Masala Sauce, Salted Cod Brandade, Mustard Greens, and Chili Onions

Sea bass	Coriander
Ginger	Cumin
Garlic	Lemon juice
Turmeric	Yogurt
Garam masala	Olive oil

1. Marinate sea bass in a mixture of ginger, garlic, turmeric, garam masala, coriander, cumin, lemon juice, yogurt, and olive oil.
2. Broil.

Tikka Masala Sauce

1	pound butter	3	ounces garam masala (available at Indian store)
1	pound yellow onions, finely chopped		
		2	cups ketchup
2	bunches cilantro, finely chopped	⅓	cup tomato paste
		4	cups chicken stock
2	serrano chilies, finely chopped	1	cup heavy cream
2	ounces ginger, chopped	½	cup sugar
2	ounces garlic, chopped		
3	ounces Kashmiri chili powder (available at Indian store)	3	ounces fenugreek leaves (available at Indian store)
			Salt and pepper to taste

1. Melt butter in saucepot.
2. Add onions, cilantro, and serrano chilies. Sauté until translucent.
3. Add ginger, garlic, chili powder, and garam masala. Sauté until aroma develops.

RECIPE CONTINUES ON NEXT PAGE

4. Add the ketchup and tomato paste and cook for about 5 minutes.

5. Add chicken stock and bring to a boil.

6. Reduce heat and simmer for about 45 minutes.

7. Add heavy cream and sugar and cook until the sauce comes back to a simmer.

8. Finish with fenugreek leaves, salt, and pepper.

Salted Cod Brandade

Salted cod	Salt and pepper
Milk	Parmesan cheese
Fresh thyme	Flour
Potatoes	Egg
Chicken stock	Breadcrumbs

1. Soak salted cod in water for 3 days.

2. Cook cod in milk and thyme in a saucepot over a low flame until totally tender.

3. Cook potatoes in chicken stock.

4. In a bowl of a stand mixer, mix the cod, cooked potatoes, salt, pepper, and Parmesan. Shape into balls.

5. Bread the salted cod balls in flour, egg wash (egg beaten with water, milk, or cream), and breadcrumbs.

Mustard Greens

Mustard greens	Chopped green chili
Spinach	Chopped cilantro
Cornmeal	Chopped tomato
Chopped onion	Coconut milk
Chopped ginger	
Chopped garlic	
Curry leaves	

1. Blanch mustard greens and spinach. Strain, squeeze out water. Chop in robot coup. Sprinkle a little cornmeal over the greens.

2. Sauté onion, ginger, garlic, curry leaves, green chili, cilantro, tomato, greens, and coconut milk together. Add mustard greens and let them cook in the coconut milk for 30 minutes.

Chili Onions

	Vidalia onions	1	tablespoon paprika
	Milk	1	tablespoon salt
1	cup flour	1	teaspoon pepper

1. Slice Vidalia onions really thin. Soak them in milk for 10 minutes.
2. Toss in a mixture of the flour, paprika, salt, and pepper.
3. Fry until crisp.

Final Assembly (in order)

1. Mustard greens
2. Sea Bass
3. Brandade
4. Tikka Masala Sauce
5. Chili Onions

Total time: 60 minutes

Ohmi Beef Tenderloin with Cipollini Onions, Oxtail Croquettes, and King Crab Oscar

Beef

Beef tenderloin

Truffle butter

Grapeseed oil

1. Cut beef tenderloin into 6 ounces pieces. Sear in a mix of truffle butter and grapeseed oil.

Cipollini Onions

Cipollini onions

Brown butter

Seasonal mushrooms

Fresh herbs

1. Pour boiling water over onions. Let sit for 10 minutes.
2. Peel the onions and toss in fresh herbs and brown butter. Roast until soft.
3. Roast mushrooms and toss with onions.

Oxtail Croquettes

Oxtail

Mashed parsnips

Butter

Flour

Egg

Breadcrumbs

1. Braise oxtails (like the short ribs). Leave in braise overnight. Shred next day.
2. Toss shredded oxtail with mashed parsnips (cook them with butter and oxtail braise sauce).
3. Form into croquettes. Bread using flour, egg wash, and breadcrumbs.

Shiraz Syrup

Shiraz wine   **Parsley**

Butter

1. Reduce shiraz and cool.
2. Mix with softened butter and parsley.

Asparagus

**Purple, white, and green
asparagus tips**

1. Blanch all.

King Crab Oscar

King crab legs   **Seasoned breadcrumbs**

Clarified butter   **Hollandaise sauce**

1. Poach crab in warm clarified butter.
2. Roll in seasoned breadcrumbs.

Final Assembly (in order)

1. Beef on left
2. Asparagus on right
3. Cipollini Onions on beef
4. Oxtail Croquette next to beef
5. King crab on top of asparagus
6. Hollandaise sauce on top of crab
7. Shiraz Syrup

Total time: 4 hours

Gingersnap Cappuccino with Candied Pecans, Cappuccino Foam, and Chocolate Miso Brûlée

Chocolate Miso Brûlée

116.4 ounces cream, warmed

1.3 pounds sugar

5.3 ounces red miso

1.7 lb. egg yolk

1.3 lb. milk chocolate

1. Mix sugar, miso, yolk. Cook to 85 degrees. Strain and pour over chocolate.
2. Add cream. Pour into cups and bake at 325 degrees for 15 to 20 minutes. Cool.

Candied Pecans

2   tablespoons unsalted butter

3   cups pecan halves

½   cup light brown sugar

½   teaspoon cinnamon

1   teaspoon kosher salt

¼   cup water

1   teaspoon vanilla extract

1. Preheat oven to 350 degrees.
2. In a skillet, melt butter and add pecans. Cook slowly to toast.
3. Add the brown sugar and stir for an additional 4 to 5 minutes over medium heat
4. Stir in the cinnamon and water.
5. Cook till water evaporates, frequently stirring.
6. Remove from heat, stir in vanilla, and spread evenly on a baking sheet.
7. Bake for 5 to 7 minutes or until fragrant and crisp.
8. Remove from oven and allow to cool on the baking sheet.

Gingersnap Vanilla Ice Cream

Vanilla ice cream   **Ground gingersnap cookies**

1. Whip ice cream with ground gingersnap cookies.

Cappuccino Foam

6   cups fresh espresso   2.2 pounds (35 ounces) milk

5.5 ounces sugar   2.2 pounds cream

20 gelatin leaves   1.8 oz Trablit liquid coffee extract

1. Warm espresso and mix in sugar. Add gelatin leaves and mix.
2. Add milk, cream and Trablit; strain.
3. Add mixture to a whipped cream dispenser and charge with whipped cream chargers.

Final Assembly (in order)

1. Cup with Chocolate Miso Brûlée
2. Candied Pecans
3. Gingersnap Vanilla Ice Cream
4. Cappuccino Foam
5. Gingersnap cookies

Time: 60 minutes

Bone Marrow Gravy

10	pounds frozen marrow bones	Cornstarch
½	box burgundy wine	Cold sherry
10	shallots	Salt and pepper as needed
1	pound mushrooms	Sugar as needed
3	carrots, roughly chopped	Beef broth
¼	bunch thyme	Bay leaves
2	gallons veal stock	Peppercorns

1. Soak thawed marrow bones in warm water.
2. Gently remove marrow and put in ice water.
3. Roast bones until dark brown.
4. In large rondeau, reduce wine, shallots, mushrooms, carrots, and thyme to 2 cups.
5. Add veal stock and roasted bones and simmer until slightly thickened.
6. Slurry with cornstarch and cold sherry. Cook 10 minutes.
7. Season with salt, pepper, and sugar.
8. To poach marrow, bring beef broth, bay leaves, and peppercorn to rolling boil, reduce heat to simmer, and poach marrow meat for 8 minutes. Cool and reserve.

Yield: 2½ gallons • Time: 2 hours

Chocolate Molten Cake

7	whole eggs	4	ounces 61% chocolate
7	egg yolks	11	ounces semisweet chocolate
1	pound sugar	4	ounces cornstarch
11	ounces butter		

1. With paddle attachment, mix whole eggs, egg yolks, and sugar.
2. In a double boiler, melt butter, 61% chocolate, and semisweet chocolate.
3. While mixing, add the melted chocolate and butter to the egg mixture.
4. Fold in cornstarch using a spatula.
5. Pour into greased molds and bake at 300 degrees for 15 minutes.

Serves 10 • Time: 45 minutes

Coconut Curry Lobster Bisque

1	pound yellow onions		1	pound lobster shells
8	ounces celery		4	ounces tomato paste
8	ounces carrot		2	ounces Thai red curry paste
4	ounces scallion		2	cups saké
4	ounces mint		2	ounces palm sugar
4	ounces basil		¼	cup lime juice
1	bunch cilantro		2	cups chicken stock
4	ounces ginger, peeled		6	cups coconut milk
4	ounces garlic cloves		⅓	cup brown sugar
2	ounces lobster base			

1. Rough chop vegetables and herbs and sauté in oil until translucent. Roast lobster shells 20 minutes.
2. Add roasted lobster shells, tomato paste, and curry paste. Cook on low for 15 minutes.
3. Add saké and reduce.
4. Add remaining ingredients and bring to simmer.
5. Cook for 1 hour.
6. Purée in blender and then pass through a chinois.

Serves 12 • Time: 2 hours

Brandy Peppercorn Sauce

3	ounces butter	12	ounces veal stock or veal demi
3	ounces shallots, finely minced	3	ounces heavy cream
6	ounces green peppercorns, drained and finely chopped	½	ounce fresh thyme
2	ounces garlic cloves, finely chopped		Salt and pepper to taste
3	ounces brandy		Lemon juice to taste

1. Melt butter in saucepan and lightly brown.
2. Add shallots and sauté until translucent.
3. Add peppercorns and sauté until aroma develops.
4. Add garlic and sauté until lightly caramelized.
5. Carefully add the brandy and light with a match. Cook out the flames.
6. Once the flames are out, add the veal stock/demi.
7. Bring sauce to a boil, turn down heat, and reduce by one-third.
8. Add the cream, thyme, salt, pepper, and lemon juice.
9. Once cream comes to a simmer, turn off flame. Taste and reserve.

Time: 45 minutes

Kung Pao Lobster

Canola oil as needed

2   eggs (use only the egg whites; reserve egg yolks for another use)

8   ounces lobster tail (cut into 5 pieces)

1   cup cornstarch

1½ cups Kung Pao Sauce

3   tablespoons finely chopped scallions (white & green)

Chili threads as needed

Crushed peanuts as needed

1. Preheat fryer with the canola oil to 325 degrees.
2. Whip egg whites until frothy.
3. Add lobster tail to the cornstarch and coat throughout.
4. Carefully coat the lobster with the egg whites.
5. Add lobster to preheated canola oil.
6. Fry until golden, about 7 to 8 minutes.
7. Remove to paper towel to absorb excess oil.
8. Place in a shallow bowl.
9. Heat Kung Pao Sauce in saucepot over medium heat until it comes to a simmer, about 5 minutes.
10. Toss the fried lobster with the Kung Pao Sauce.
11. Sprinkle with chopped scallions, chili threads, and crushed peanuts.

Serves 5 • Time: 60 minutes

Kung Pao Sauce

1 cup tomato ketchup

½ cup soy sauce

⅓ cup sambal paste

¼ cup rice vinegar

⅓ cup sugar

3 tablespoons scallions (white and green), finely chopped

2 tablespoons ginger, peeled and finely chopped

Salt & pepper to taste

1. Mix all ingredients in a mixing bowl.
2. Taste for seasoning and set aside.

Ricotta Cheesecake

Ricotta cheese must be drained in refrigerator overnight (at least 8 hours). To drain the ricotta, line a fine-mesh sieve with 2 layers of paper towels, place cheese in the sieve, place sieve over a bowl, and then refrigerate.

Crust

1¼ cups graham cookie crust crumbs

4 tablespoons unsalted butter, melted, plus additional

1 tablespoon melted unsalted butter for greasing pan

Ricotta Filling

2 pounds ricotta cheese, drained overnight (see above draining instructions)

4 large eggs, separated

¾ cup sugar

¼ cup sherry

1 tablespoon unbleached all-purpose flour

Grated lemon zest (from 1 lemon)

2 teaspoons vanilla extract

⅛ teaspoon table salt

1. Crust: Adjust oven rack to lower-middle position and heat to 325 degrees. In small bowl, combine graham crumbs and melted butter. Toss with fork until evenly moistened. Brush bottom and sides of 9-inch springform pan with most of the remaining tablespoon of melted butter, reserving small amount of excess melted butter for brushing sides of pan after crust cools. Empty crumbs into springform pan and press evenly into pan bottom. Bake until fragrant and beginning to brown around edges (about 13 minutes.) Cool on wire rack to room temperature (about 30 minutes). Do not turn off oven. Brush sides of springform pan with remaining melted butter.

2. Ricotta Filling: While crust cools, place drained ricotta in food processor and process until very smooth (about 1 minute). Add egg yolks, sugar, sherry, flour, zest, vanilla, and salt and process until blended (about 1 more minute). Scrape mixture into large bowl.

3. In the bowl of a stand mixer, beat egg whites at high speed until they hold stiff peaks. Fold whites into ricotta mixture until fully incorporated and pour mixture evenly into cooled crust.

4. Bake cheesecake until top is lightly browned and an instant-read thermometer inserted into the center registers about 150 degrees (about 1¼ hours.) Perimeter of cake should be firm, but center will jiggle slightly. It will solidify further as cake cools. Transfer pan to wire rack and cool for 5 minutes. Run paring knife between cake and side of springform pan. Cool until barely warm (about 2½ to 3 hours). Wrap pan tightly in plastic wrap and refrigerate until cheesecake is cold and set (at least 5 hours but up to 2 days).
5. To unmold cheesecake, remove sides of pan. Let cheesecake stand at room temperature for about 30 minutes. Cut into wedges and serve.

Serves 8 to 10 • Time: 2.5 hours

Family recipes from my mother and foremost teacher, Taru Dhurandhar

Coffee Montana

1	egg white	¼	cup sugar
2	tablespoons sugar	1	tablespoon coffee powder
1	cup chopped toasted almonds	1	teaspoon vanilla extract
¼	cup desiccated coconut		Few drops almond extract
1	cup cream		

1. Beat egg white until soft peaks form.
2. Gradually add 2 tablespoons sugar and beat until stiff.
3. Combine almonds and coconut.
4. Whip the cream, fold in ¼ cup sugar, coffee powder, and flavorings.
5. Fold in the beaten egg white and half of the nut mixture.
6. Pour this into a tray and sprinkle the remaining nut mixture over it.
7. Freeze until firm.
8. Thaw and serve hot.

Serves 2 to 4 • Time: 1 hour

Apple Torte

2	cups chopped unpeeled apples	½	tablespoon melted butter
½	cup sugar	½	teaspoon vanilla extract
¼	cup flour	¼	cup chopped walnuts
1	teaspoon baking powder	¼	cup chopped dates
1	small egg		

1. Combine ingredients and mix well.
2. Transfer to greased baking dish.
3. Bake in a hot oven at 400 degrees for 40 minutes.
4. Serve warm with fresh cream or ice cream.

Serves 4 to 6 • Time: 1.5 hours

Shrimp Dejonge

¼ cup melted butter

4 cloves garlic, finely chopped

1 tablespoon chopped parsley or coriander leaves

2 tablespoons sherry

½ teaspoon chili powder

Pepper and salt to taste

¼ cup soft breadcrumbs

2 cups cooked prawns

1. In a bowl, mix the melted butter, garlic, parsley, sherry, chili powder, pepper, and salt together.
2. Add the breadcrumbs and toss.
3. Arrange the cooked prawns in a baking dish. Spoon the breadcrumb mixture on top.
4. Bake in a preheated 360-degree oven until the crumbs are golden brown. Serve hot.

Serves 2 to 4 • Time: 1 hour

Stuffed Masala Eggs

2   tablespoons grated fresh coconut

½   inch piece ginger

6   cloves garlic

2   tablespoons vegetable oil

1   large onion, finely chopped

1   medium tomato, finely chopped

½   teaspoon turmeric power

2   teaspoon chili powder

Salt to taste

6   eggs, boiled, shelled, and cut into halves; yolks removed and chopped

1   tablespoon finely chopped coriander leaves

1. Grind coconut, ginger, and garlic to a fine paste.
2. Heat vegetable oil in a pan. Fry onion in oil until golden brown.
3. Add chopped tomato. Fry for one minute. Add coconut paste, turmeric, chili powder, and salt. Sauté lightly.
4. Add chopped egg yolks and coriander leaves.
5. Fill egg whites with the above mixture.
6. Heat a small amount of oil in another pan. Add the stuffed eggs. Cook for 5 minutes.
7. Serve eggs in a dish lined with cucumber and tomato slices and sprinkled with coriander leaves.

Time: 1 hour

Palak Mutton

½ teaspoon turmeric powder

1 teaspoon chili powder

¼ teaspoon garam masala

¼ cup curds

½ tablespoon vegetable oil

Green Masala Paste (below)

16 to 19 ounces mutton

3 onions, thinly sliced

3 tablespoons vegetable oil

1 bunch spinach, cleaned and finely chopped

2 tomatoes, finely chopped

1 quart water

½ cup cashews, ground to a paste

1. Clean and rinse the mutton.
2. Add turmeric power, chili powder, garam masala, curds, and ½ tablespoon vegetable oil to 1 cup of the Green Masala Paste. Mix well. Marinate the mutton in the mixture for 2 to 3 hours.
3. Fry the onions in 3 tablespoons vegetable oil until golden brown.
4. Add the spinach. Fry for another minute or so and then do the same with the tomatoes.
5. Add the marinated mutton and 1 quart water. Cook until tender. Add the cashew paste and remaining Green Masala Paste. Bring to a boil, turn down heat, and let simmer for 10 minutes.

Green Masala Paste

6 green chilis

½ cup coriander leaves

1 tablespoon mint leaves

1 (2-inch) piece ginger

1 clove garlic

1. Process the ingredients in a blender until a paste forms.

Serves 2 to 4 • Time: 3 hours

About the Author

Award-winning chef Samir Dhurandhar has anchored the high-energy kitchen at internationally acclaimed Nick & Sam's steakhouse in Dallas since its founding in 1999.

A native of India, the restaurant's partner and corporate chef grew up in Bombay (Mumbai) as a fledgling "sous chef" under the wing of his mother, Taru, a cooking instructor known for her culinary mastery throughout the Juhu section of the huge international city. From his mother's early influence, Samir learned both the art of flavor and the skill of cultural infusion that he skillfully carries forth today with a passionate, distinctive flair. At the age of thirteen, he was cooking for friends and family.

Samir launched his professional career as a junior sous chef at the India Sheraton. On a family trip to the US, he met cooking legend Julia Child, who encouraged him to attend the prestigious Culinary Institute of America in Hyde Park, New York.

Upon graduation, Samir landed a prominent post at the trendy Sfuzzi in Manhattan, where he would become the first executive chef in the chain to create his own menu. He created innovative menus for John Harvard's Brewhouse in Long Island and the Heartland Brewery Restaurant Group as well. Samir has cooked for Sign of the Dove and the Robert De Niro–owned Tribeca Grill, among other notable Big Apple dining venues.

Soon after his arrival at Nick & Sam's, Samir won the American Institute of Wine and Food's 2000 Upcoming Chef Award and has gone on to capture a litany of honors in his twenty-four years at the restaurant. He also built menus for several concepts created by Nick & Sam's founder and industry legend, Phil Romano, including The Network Bar.

In 2016, Samir garnered the ultimate industry honor when he was invited to cook at the prestigious James Beard House in New York. Previously, Samir and his Nick & Sam's staff had won the International Five Star Diamond Award.

The chef, who in 2021 launched a gourmet catering service, Savor by Samir, has been profiled in *Haute Living, D Magazine, Texas Monthly,* the *Dallas Morning News,* and dozens of other publications and websites. He also has made numerous television appearances on network and regional shows.

Samir, his wife, Lori, and their children, Mia and Cole, live in Dallas.

Index

RECIPE LISTING

Allen Brothers Prime Filet and Bluefin Toro with Caviar, Truffles, and Pickled Fresno Chiles, 131

Apple Fennel Slaw, 125

Apple Torte, 151

Asparagus, 139

Australian Wagyu Short Rib Cannelloni with Reggiano Fonduta and San Marzano Tomatoes, 132

Barbecued Beef Bacon, 124

Bone Marrow Gravy, 142

Brandy Peppercorn Sauce, 145

Brown Butter Croutons, 134

Candied Pecans, 140

Cappuccino Foam, 141

Chicken Liver Crostini, 128

Chicken Liver Mousse, 128

Chilean Sea Bass with Tikka Masala Sauce, Salted Cod Brandade, Mustard Greens, and Chili Onions, 135

Chili Onions, 137

Chocolate Miso Brûlée, 140

Chocolate Molten Cake, 143

Cipollini Onions, 138

Coconut Curry Lobster Bisque, 144

Coffee Montana, 150

Crab Cake Poppers, 127

Crespelle, 132

Crisp Eggs, 134

Crispy Oyster Gougères with Barbecued Beef Bacon, 124

Crispy Oysters, 124

Dijon Vinaigrette, 134

Eggplant Papadum, 130

Gingersnap Cappuccino with Candied Pecans, Cappuccino Foam, and Chocolate Miso Brûlée, 140

Gingersnap Vanilla Ice Cream, 141

Gougères, 125

Green Masala Paste, 154

King Crab Oscar, 139

Kung Pao Lobster, 146

Kung Pao Sauce, 147

Little Gem Caesar Salad with Crisp Eggs and Bottarga, 134

Mustard Greens, 136

Ohmi Beef Tenderloin with Cipollini Onions, Oxtail Croquettes, and King Crab Oscar, 138

Oxtail Croquettes, 138

Palak Mutton, 154

Pickled Fresno Chilies, 131

Port Jelly, 129

Reggiano Fonduta, 133

Ricotta Cheesecake, 148

Salted Cod Brandade, 136

Shiraz Syrup, 139

Short Ribs, 132

Shrimp Dejonge, 152

Smokra Aïoli, 126

Stuffed Masala Eggs, 153

Tarragon Vinaigrette, 125

Tikka Masala Sauce, 135

Tomato Preserves, 127

Tomato Shallot Compote, 133

RECIPES BY SECTION
Family Recipes
Apple Torte, 151

Coffee Montana, 150

Palak Mutton, 154

Shrimp Dejonge, 152

Stuffed Masala Eggs, 153

James Beard House Dinner Recipes
Allen Brothers Prime Filet and Bluefin
  Toro with Caviar, Truffles, and Pickled
  Fresno Chiles, 131

Australian Wagyu Short Rib Cannelloni
  with Reggiano Fonduta and San
  Marzano Tomatoes, 132

Chicken Liver Crostini, 128

Chilean Sea Bass with Tikka Masala
  Sauce, Salted Cod Brandade, Mustard
  Greens, and Chili Onions, 135

Crab Cake Poppers, 127

Crispy Oyster Gougères with Barbecued
  Beef Bacon, 124

Eggplant Papadum, 130

Gingersnap Cappuccino with Candied
  Pecans, Cappuccino Foam, and
  Chocolate Miso Brûlée, 140

Little Gem Caesar Salad with Crisp Eggs
  and Bottarga, 134

Ohmi Beef Tenderloin with Cipollini
  Onions, Oxtail Croquettes, and King
  Crab Oscar, 138

Nick & Sam's Favorites
Bone Marrow Gravy, 142

Brandy Peppercorn Sauce, 145

Chocolate Molten Cake, 143

Coconut Curry Lobster Bisque, 144

Kung Pao Lobster, 146

Ricotta Cheesecake, 148